THE
Believer's
Guide
TO
Legal Issues

The
Believer's Guide
To
Legal Issues

Lacey,
May this be a blessing to
you!

Psalm 127:1

STEPHEN BLOOM

LIVING
INK
BOOKS
Writing Worth Reading

First printing—April 2008
Cover designed by Meyer's Design, Houston, Texas
Interior design and typesetting by Reider Publishing Services, West Hollywood, California
Edited and Proofread by Rich Cairnes, Dan Penwell, Sharon Neal, and Rick Steele

Printed in the United States of America
14 13 12 11 10 09 08 –CH– 7 6 5 4 3 2 1

Library of Congress Cataloging-in-Publication Data

Bloom, Stephen L., 1961-
    The believer's guide to legal issues / Stephen L. Bloom.
        p. cm.
    Summary: "A Christian lawyer offers practical, helpful advice along with God's bibli-
cal counsel to bring hope, healing, and peace to Christian believers facing everyday legal
situations. The legal topics addressed are carefully selected and include very hot topics
like living wills, living trusts, medical assistance planning, bankruptcy, divorce, taxes, and
litigation"—Provided by publisher.
    ISBN 978-0-89957-031-0 (pbk. : alk. paper) 1. Religion and law. 2. Law--United
States--Popular works. I. Title.
    BL65.L33B56 2008
    349.73024'27—dc22   2008005839

Contents

With love, to Sharon,
truly the best wife a guy could ever be blessed with

For the glory of God

Acknowledgments

Thus is the man blessed who fears the LORD.

—PSALM 128:4

God, for making all things possible.

My lovely wife, Sharon, for all the times you've patiently listened, for all your amazing wisdom, for all your encouragement, for all your love, for all your beauty, for all your support. I would be nowhere in life, spiritually or otherwise, without you. You are the most precious to me.

My awesome kids, Nick, Anna, and Katy, for making this whole adventure we call life so fun and worthwhile. Being your dad brings me honor and joy beyond measure.

My parents and grandparents.

My professional mentors, William F. Martson, Esquire, and Ivo V. Otto III, Esquire, for your irreplaceable guidance; Lori Hoffman and all the other wonderful legal support staff I've been privileged to work with over the years; my professional colleagues; my Messiah College students; and my clients, past, present, and future.

My faithful team at AMG Publishers/Living Ink Books, especially Dan Penwell for seeing the potential in this project, Rich Cairnes for patiently translating so much of my legalese into English, and Sharon Neal for her discerning eye in catching proofreading issues that few other people would see.

My beloved Grace United Methodist Church family and my pastors during the course of this writing, Rev. Dr. Marlin Snider, Rev. Eric Shafer, Rev. Sharonn Halderman, Pastor Ed D'Agostino, and Rev. Bruce Fensterbush, just for being my pastors (you have the hardest job of all!).

Foreword

The proverb that says an "ounce of prevention is worth a pound of cure" aptly describes the true value of the "practical counsel" the reader will find on every page of Steve Bloom's very helpful book. Best of all, Mr. Bloom's experienced counsel is not just practical, it is eternal—because it soundly rests on the words of God as set forth in Holy Scripture.

Having practiced law for more than thirty years, I find collected in this book just the sort of sage advice I would give to my dearest friend or closest relative. I imagine that if taken to heart this book might save the reader much heartache, not to mention wasted time and unnecessary legal fees.

It is no secret that Christians in America divorce just as often as nonbelievers and are involved in more than four million lawsuits annually. Indeed, it can be whimsically stated that where two or more Christians are gathered together in Jesus' name, there all too often is conflict. Rather than resolve these conflicts within the church, too many Christians are sent to attorneys and courthouses where they never hear the good advice found on the pages of this book.

On the other hand, here at the Christian Legal Society (www .clsnet.org), we know from the fact that we provide more than

10,000 legal referrals to the public every year, most people do not know how to (1) find a good attorney they can truly trust, or (2) how to properly evaluate the moral value of the advice they are receiving from the legal counsel they *do* retain. A reading of this book will better prepare anyone to wisely retain and best work with their legal counsel.

Mr. Bloom's wise and Christ-honoring approach to identifying, understanding, and responding to the legal problems most commonly faced by Americans today is a useful drink of water for a thirsty church. Best of all, the book sets forth in general terms just the sort of moral considerations we all should hear and understand before investing considerable time and money in unnecessary legal proceedings—proceedings that may only result in us kissing our most important relationships good-bye.

Mr. Bloom's book not only shows folks facing legal problems how to best respond to those problems. It also serves to provide Christian lawyers and law students with a good example of how they might better advise their clients.

Of course there is no better example of a Christian lawyer than Jesus. First John 2:1 says: "If anybody does sin, we have one who speaks to the Father in our defense—Jesus Christ, the Righteous One." The "we" John refers to in this passage are people he knew to be followers of Christ, those who by their confession of faith had already "retained" Jesus as their advocate or attorney to represent them, defend them, and even stand in their place before the judgment seat of God. No "client" of Jesus has ever or will ever receive ineffective representation. None of Jesus' clients has ever lost his or her case for salvation before the throne of heaven. Even the guilty thief crucified with Jesus, when he asked Jesus to remember him in heaven, found the dying Jesus to be a caring and effective advocate.

According to Scripture, those in eternal torment are so because they decided or preferred to represent themselves (or sought some advocate, argument, or thing other than Jesus) to make their case for righteousness before an all-holy and all-righteous God. Not one of those in eternal torment is Jesus' client. Their unfortunate ends are as predictable as that of the guilty criminal defendant who decides to represent himself and has no one to take his punishment for him.

It is true that Jesus had some harsh criticisms for the lawyers of his day who were always trying "to oppose him fiercely and to besiege him with questions, waiting to catch him in something he might say" (Luke 11:53–54). However, a careful reading of Luke 11:42 demonstrates Jesus cared about right practice of law. He was actually providing a job description for a lawyer who follows God, in contradiction to the legalistic, egocentric, hypocritical lawyers of his day. Those lawyers were focusing on trivialities and forgetting justice, truth, and fair treatment of others—characteristics often applied to lawyers today. For Jesus, a Christian lawyer would not forget the "weightier matters of the law"—justice, mercy, and faithfulness (Matthew 23:23).

Read this useful book. Whether you are seeking Christian legal counsel or trying to provide it, this book will help you bear in mind those "weightier matters of the law" that Jesus encourages all of us to always remember—justice, mercy, and faithfulness.

Sam

Samuel B. Casey
Executive Director and CEO
Christian Legal Society
8001 Braddock Road, *Suite 300*
Springfield, Virginia 22151
703-642-1070, Ext. 3201 (*office*)
703-642-1075 (*facsimile*)
703-624-4092 (*mobile*)
sbcasey@clsnet.org
www.clsnet.org

Preface

Unless the LORD builds the house,
its builders labor in vain.

—PSALM 127:1

It was a summer night in Philadelphia, July 10, 1998. My knees ached against the concrete as I prayed, wedged between the front of my own folded stadium seat and the seatbacks of the row below.

The space wasn't designed for prayer. Perfect, maybe, for standing to cheer a touchdown run or a long drive to deep left field, but not an ideal place for a grown man to drop to his knees and pray. Yet there I was, with 40,000 of my brothers in Christ, all kneeling awkwardly but reverently, in silence on the stadium floor.

I had been struggling intensely for almost a year, wrestling with God over a major decision. As the weekend of the Promise Keepers stadium conference approached, I prayed that God would somehow use this event to answer my prayers, to reveal his will to me in a clear, understandable way.

Even on the hundred-mile bus ride to the stadium, I continued to pray that this might be the weekend. Still, I wasn't prepared for the speed or clarity with which God would speak to me that night in Philadelphia.

It was only the first evening of the two-day conference. The man who asked us to get on our knees was only the first of more than a half dozen speakers lined up for the weekend. And yet, as he led us in those moments of prayer, there it was.

It wasn't something the speaker said. It wasn't an audible voice. It wasn't even phrased as a direct response to the question I'd been wrestling with. But it was totally clear, almost insistent in its clarity. It was the unmistakable voice of God. The words were as thunderous as they were quiet. I had my answer: "YOU KNOW WHAT YOU HAVE TO DO."

I'd been a born-again believer in Jesus Christ for nearly nine years and a practicing lawyer for almost eleven. At first, the two seemed entirely compatible. But as the Holy Spirit steadily cleansed my heart over the years, a tension gradually began to build. By 1997, that tension was maturing into a full-blown spiritual crisis. Could I, as a Christian, continue to make my living in a profession that seemed to embrace a value system entirely contrary to the teachings of Jesus?

So I began to pray and struggle. I was a partner in one of the largest and most well-respected law firms in our county. The men and women I worked with were good, honest, and decent folks. Many were even Christians. The financial compensation was excellent and the future, by all accounts, was secure. But it was a secular firm practicing law from the same worldly perspective as a thousand other firms across the country. Nothing illegal or improper, but certainly no intentional focus on incorporating Christian values into legal practice.

On one hand, I sensed God calling me to do something radical. While I had a good measure of freedom at the law firm, still there were unspoken rules of conformity and a conventional secular approach was expected. The firm was simply not the place to experiment with an entirely new way of practicing law. Further, it wasn't yet clear to me whether God was actually calling me to become a "Christian lawyer" or if he was, instead, calling me to leave the legal profession altogether for a ministerial vocation.

On the other hand, I had a wife and three young children to support. Did it make sense to put them at economic risk to pursue a somewhat vague and uncertain path? And if I left the law firm, wouldn't that be taking the easy way out? Shouldn't I just buck up and try to be a witness for Christ where I was?

The questions kept multiplying. Would leaving the firm be disloyal to my partners? Or would staying on when my heart was elsewhere actually be more disloyal? Was it possible to become an overtly Christian lawyer, or would I merely be trading on the name of Christ for financial gain? Could I even make a living at all as a Christian lawyer? My mind was racing. What did God really want me to do? Many times over I'd convince myself to hold steady on the course, only to find all the questions rushing back within months, or weeks, or even days.

By early 1998, I was beginning to drive my very patient wife and myself to frustration. At some point, she temporarily "banned" me from discussing the topic with her any further, to give us a much-needed break. But as the year slipped by and the date for that summer's Promise Keepers event eased closer, I began to gain a sense of hope that perhaps, at long last, a decision would finally be at hand.

And so it was that I found myself listening to God speak to me that hot July night in Veterans Stadium in Philadelphia. The uncertainty and doubt had been instantaneously removed. Thanks be to God, I knew what I had to do. From that night on, it was simply a matter of finding the courage to do it. I would start a Christian law practice.

And when the time was right, God filled me with the courage I needed. There were some inevitable tears and a few heated discussions, but all in all, the transition unfolded as if God's hand was directing the entire process, which I believe it was. My professional associates conducted themselves with admirable class and integrity, for which I will always remain grateful, and my clients responded with a level of support beyond anything I had imagined possible.

So, in keeping with God's incomparable sense of humor and timing, I launched my new law practice on April Fools' Day 1999, sailing faithfully into an unknown realm under the hopeful banner "Practical Counsel—Christian Perspective."

Over the years since, I have worked and prayed to discover a truly Christian perspective on the law, and to discern biblical principles with practical application to the real-life situations faced by my clients. I have encountered some successes and some failures. Through my own weakness, I have missed many opportunities to glorify God. But in humbling myself before him, I have also been privileged to participate in some miraculous demonstrations of God's strength and power. Being a sinner, saved only by God's grace, I expect that the future will hold more of the same.

I offer this book to share some of the things I've learned so far. I pray that it will be an encouragement to the body of believers to live out the abundant life God promises. And I pray that it will serve as a warning to help us avoid some of the many traps and snares Satan has set for us in the legal system (a glimpse of hell itself in the minds of many reading this, I am sure!). Although written for nonlawyers, I trust that my fellow attorneys will be enlightened as well. I have encountered too many lawyers who publicly present themselves as Christians, but in practice are virtually indistinguishable from their secular peers. I believe God has something much better in mind for all of us.

May this book be a blessing to you.

Stephen L. Bloom, Esquire
Carlisle, Pennsylvania

Introduction

Everyone who does evil hates the light, and will not come into
the light for fear that his deeds will be exposed. But whoever lives
by the truth comes into the light, so that it may be seen plainly
that what he has done has been done through God.

—JOHN 3:20–21

I have divided each chapter into several segments. First, there
are two fictional vignettes—"Life Lessons" and "More Life Lessons"—showing some potential consequences of either ignoring or applying biblical principles to everyday legal situations. This
is followed by "Biblical Insights." Here I list Scripture passages relevant to the topic under consideration. Often many additional
Scripture passages could have been included—my listings are illus-
trative, not exhaustive. Each chapter concludes with "Practical
Counsel," representing my own thoughts on how and why we
might apply the principles in question to our lives as Christians.

The segments are intended to complement one another. It's
my hope that through the combination of the three approaches

the reader will become reasonably well informed about the principles being discussed.

The person who likes to learn in the context of a story might connect best with "Life Lessons" and "More Life Lessons" in each chapter. Someone who says, "Just show me the Scripture" will probably benefit most from "Biblical Insights." The reader who prefers an explanatory approach will relate more to "Practical Counsel." But I would strongly recommend reading the entire book for maximum impact, as none of the segments is intended to stand alone. I believe that the three approaches in concert will best facilitate the integration of the biblical wisdom into your hearts.

Finally, I must offer the standard lawyer's disclaimer that this book is not intended to be a substitute for legal advice provided by your own attorney. Each person's circumstances are unique and may require expert professional evaluation. I would encourage the reader to seek out a competent Christian attorney willing to share his or her testimony of salvation and able to intelligently explain the reconciliation of his or her faith with the practice of law. And please consider passing a copy of this book along to your lawyer. I am convinced a tremendous healing would begin in our society if more lawyers were empowered to apply Christian principles in the day-to-day practice of law.

CHAPTER 1

The Litigation Trap

A man's wisdom gives him patience;
it is to his glory to overlook an offense.
—PROVERBS 19:11

Life Lessons—Jeff and Jenny

Jeff slowly ran his fingers through Jenny's soft blonde hair as he climbed back into bed after closing the bedroom windows.

"Just try to get some sleep, Jen. We've been through so much lately, and you worked so late tonight," he whispered gently. Though Jeff's words sounded reassuring, silently he was asking himself, *Could it be true?*

Jenny's tired voice quivered, "I can't sleep up here, Jeff." He could tell she was exhausted and close to tears. His heart sank as she slid out of bed. He knew what was coming next. "With the windows shut, I'll never fall asleep anyway—it's too stuffy," she grumbled, pulling on her cloth robe. "I'll have to sleep downstairs on the couch as usual."

And then, with an unmistakable edge in her voice, "I thought that big shot lawyer of yours was going to get this problem solved. Instead, it gets worse every night. A real husband would stand up for his family. Why don't you go next door and tell those people off once and for all?" It was never like Jenny to be so harsh. As she stormed down the steps, everything became too clear to Jeff.

"My gosh," he muttered, "what have I gotten us into?"

Even with the windows locked tight, Jeff could hear the steady beat of the drums and bass guitar rattling against the glass as he lay there alone in the dark bedroom. The houses were so close. It was only 10:30 and it was going to be another long and lonely night. *How has it come to this?* he lamented. Now it seemed like even his relationship with Jenny had fallen apart. *God, I hate those people!* he seethed.

As he drifted fitfully in and out of sleep, Jeff recounted events in his mind. Life had been good before those people moved in. At first, he and Jenny had intended to invite them over for a cookout some weekend, to get to know them and welcome them to the neighborhood. But with tight work schedules and running the kids around to day care and activities, it just never got on the calendar. That was all before the music started.

Well, at least we did one thing right, Jeff reflected emptily. *I'm glad we never invited those jerks onto our property.*

The first time the music came on next door, it wasn't such a big deal. Jeff figured that maybe they were throwing a little party or something. Sleep came easily enough without the anger. But after the third night in a row Jenny, he, and the kids were all getting agitated. Jeff was the man of the house and he was going to have to do something. He thought about going next door and asking them to turn the music down, but he had no idea how they might react. It was late, and he especially didn't like the looks of the neighbor's teenage son. He feared things could get ugly. That's when he thought of calling the police.

It seemed like the perfect solution. It was the safe thing to do and nobody would even have to know who called in the complaint. The officers showed up next door about twenty minutes later and things got quiet instantly. Soon everyone settled down and fell asleep.

But the next night, the music was back. So the police were called again. "If that's what it takes, that's what we'll do," Jeff said stubbornly. "I'll call them every night if I have to." And the cycle continued for the rest of the week.

That Saturday morning, it was bright and sunny and Jenny went out to wash the car while working on her tan. But soon she noticed the neighbors staring at her and whispering among themselves. After a few minutes, she felt so uncomfortable she went back inside, still wet and soapy, without finishing the car.

"Those people are strange," she said to Jeff. "They're just staring at me."

Jeff looked at her skeptically, laughing it off, and quipped, "Jen, you do look good in that bikini, but you're probably just imagining that people are staring at you."

That Sunday, unwelcome trash started to appear. An empty can. A food wrapper. Jeff and Jenny began finding litter in their backyard almost every day. They never saw anyone put it there, but it kept appearing. Jeff started getting concerned.

By then, Jeff wasn't thinking twice about calling the police as soon as the music started up each night. But one night after he called, there was a knock on his own front door.

"Are you Jeff Johnson?" the young police corporal asked him. Jeff nodded. "Mr. Johnson, we've been called to the house next door every night for over a week now. I did some checking back at the station. We have a noise ordinance on the books, but the music next door isn't quite loud enough to violate our law." Jeff listened with a puzzled look. "From now on, Mr. Johnson," the corporal continued, "we're going to consider it a civil matter."

Jeff eyed the officer for a moment, then snapped sharply, "Well, what am *I* supposed to do?"

The officer shrugged his shoulders and replied, "I guess you'd better call your lawyer." That was more than two months ago, Jeff now recalled woefully, the first night Jenny started sleeping on the couch. And when the police stopped coming every night, it seemed like the music played louder and longer, almost as if the neighbors were gloating.

The meeting with the lawyer took about a week to schedule. He was an attorney recommended by one of Jeff's friends, supposed to be very hard-nosed, which sounded good to Jeff.

Jenny and Jeff both had to arrange time off work to attend the appointment. To make matters worse, a surprisingly high initial retainer had to be charged to their overworked credit card before the lawyer would even agree to see them. Meanwhile, the music continued every night and the stress built.

The lawyer's office was dimly lit and formal. And the lawyer himself looked the part, with his dark suit and graying hair. After hearing Jeff and Jenny tell their story, the lawyer soberly advised them to avoid any contact with the neighbors, as he knew from experience that confrontations could get out of control and even become physical.

"Instead," he said dryly, "I'll send them a little nasty-gram. I think it will get their attention."

Another week passed before Jeff received a courtesy copy of the lawyer's letter, as mailed to the neighbors. His face flushed with satisfaction as he eagerly tore open the envelope and read the words the lawyer had assembled. There were threats and demands and insulting characterizations. All the sorts of things Jeff dreamed of saying to the neighbors himself if he ever confronted them, plus some complicated legal jargon that sounded very impressive. For the first time in weeks, Jeff looked forward to evening. *Jenny will be back upstairs and we'll be able to live our lives again,* he thought to himself with a little smile. *This letter will end this mess once and for all.*

That night when the music kicked on louder and earlier than ever, Jeff and Jenny looked at each other in shocked dismay. The whole family was suffering from the nightly disruption now, and with the new school year about to start, they just couldn't take much more. Jeff's fingers trembled as he dialed the lawyer's number, ready to demand immediate action. Instead, an after-hours voice-mail service advised that regular office hours were Monday through Friday from 9 to 4, and provided a menu of messaging options, none of which promised any response whatsoever. It was yet another miserable night.

Again, it took about a week to schedule an appointment with the lawyer. Again, Jeff and Jenny had to juggle their work schedules. And again, the lawyer was asking for money. "It looks like we'll have to litigate," he said gravely. "I'll need an additional retainer and I can have the court papers ready to file within a week of payment."

Over her lunch hour, Jenny reluctantly closed out the special bank account she had started back in January with hopes of providing the family with a debt-free Christmas this year. It wasn't to be. She brought the money withdrawn from the account to the lawyer's office to pay the retainer. And meanwhile, Jeff had no inkling of the situation that would begin developing later that afternoon.

When Jenny finally got back to work, Pete, a new guy from the accounting department, was waiting in her cubicle for some software training she was supposed to supervise.

"No offense, Jenny," he said, "but you look awful. Is everything okay?"

At first Jenny had no intention of sharing the details of her circumstances with Pete, but even as she tried to give him a quick overview, her tears and her words started to flow uncontrollably. He seemed to listen so intently, and he seemed so optimistic and cheerful. Just being there talking with him was making her feel better.

Lately it had become so hard for her to talk with Jeff. He was resentful of her sleeping downstairs, and he was gradually slipping into an obsession with watching the neighbors, trying desperately to catch them in the act of throwing trash into the backyard. Now he was talking about setting up surveillance cameras on the roof of the house. It was starting to get weird and she feared for Jeff's emotional well-being.

When Jenny and Pete finally got back to the software training, it was almost the end of the workday. "How about if the two of us go get a quick dinner somewhere and then stop over at my apartment to finish the training?" Pete suggested casually. "You can even stay over if you want, maybe have a quiet night's sleep for once?"

Jenny was shocked at how long she hesitated before finally mumbling, "No, I can't do that." A chill went up her spine. *Have things really gotten this bad?* she asked herself, her heart racing.

Finally, a week after the additional retainer was paid, the lawyer's secretary called Jeff to tell him the official court papers for the lawsuit were ready to be filed, as promised. It was time, Jeff proudly announced to the family, "for justice to be done." Even though he had fallen behind on some major work assignments, Jeff called in sick to the office on the day the papers were to be served by the sheriff's deputies. This would be too good to miss. He had to see the looks on the neighbors' faces when the deputies knocked on their door. In fact, he decided, he had to capture the whole thing on his new high-end video system, bought on credit just in time for the show.

Even after the papers were served, Jeff was so captivated with tracking the movements and activities of the neighbors that he wasn't especially bothered when the music started up louder than ever that evening. He knew it was only a matter of time. Soon the judge would set things straight.

And he wasn't even troubled when Jenny called from work late the next afternoon and told him she had a big project to finish and would have to stay late at the office, maybe even overnight. After all, he was perfectly capable of getting the kids dinner and putting them to bed, and then he planned to spend the rest of his evening going through catalogues featuring night-vision surveillance equipment and decibel meters. He wanted to gather some hard evidence for his day in court.

It had been a rough couple of months for him, Jenny, and the kids, but Jeff knew things were finally looking up. Their long ordeal was almost over. Or so he thought.

Now, as Jeff tossed and turned in the lonely darkness of the bedroom, it was still difficult for him to believe the shocking turn of events that began to unfold this morning, when the lawyer's secretary called him at work to say the lawyer needed an immediate consultation in light of significant developments in the case. Jeff scrambled to clear his schedule, canceling a meeting with an important customer.

When Jeff sat down across the big desk from the lawyer, the attorney's words confused him. "Counterclaim . . . malicious prosecution . . . invasion of privacy . . . harassment . . . ethnic intimidation . . . wiretapping . . . punitive damages . . . temporary injunction . . . protection from abuse order . . . criminal referral . . . district attorney's office . . . unanticipated turn of events." Jeff could feel the beads of sweat forming on his forehead.

"What in God's name is going on?" Jeff demanded. "What are you talking about?"

The lawyer began an emotionless and detached explanation that Jeff could barely follow. The lawsuit he and Jenny filed had prompted a formal counterclaim by the neighbors. The neighbors had retained an aggressive young lawyer. The young hired gun had checked through the police reports and discovered all the telephone complaints, plus the fact the music was never actually established to be in violation of the noise ordinance. The neighbors had also hired a private detective, and he had pictures of Jeff spying into their windows from the roof and lurking around their property with a video camera.

It appeared as though Jeff had even been caught trying to listen in on their conversations and telephone calls with special devices. And, it just so happened, the neighbors were recent legal immigrants and believed that Jeff's activities were part of a calculated effort to force them out of the neighborhood because of their ethnic background. And not only was it possible that significant civil damages could be assessed against Jeff and Jenny, but the local district attorney was quite interested in the whole matter and had opened a formal criminal investigation of Jeff. The lawyer then informed Jeff there was something else the private detective had captured on camera, something not actually included in the formal legal papers.

"That's it, forget it!" Jeff finally announced to the lawyer after a moment of stunned silence. "I give up—I'm withdrawing our lawsuit. We're not going to continue this. This has to end right now. Our family cannot deal with all this."

For the first time during any of their meetings, the lawyer actually looked at Jeff with a trace of emotion on his face, an expression of sympathy it appeared. Then he spoke very slowly, in a strange and different tone. "Jeff, I don't think you understand. We cannot stop this now. The counterclaim has been filed. The criminal investigation is underway. You could lose everything you own. You could go to jail. It is now beyond our control. All we can do is prepare our defense."

Again, there was a period of stunned silence as Jeff tried to grasp the implications of the unthinkable reversal. This time the lawyer's words broke the quiet. "Jeff," he said, "I'll need to double my retainer. I need payment immediately. And that may be just the beginning." Jeff gasped and shifted in his seat, unable to say anything.

Then the lawyer spoke again. "Jeff, do you know where Jenny spent last Thursday evening?"

Jeff dragged himself home in a cloud of disbelief and confusion. *How can I tell Jenny what's happening? Or does she even care anymore? Can the information from the private detective about Jenny possibly be true? Are there really pictures of her with another man on Thursday night? It just can't be,* he convinced himself. *If only Jenny and I can be like a normal husband and wife again, things will be fine and we can deal with these legal problems together. I'll have to break it to her slowly at first. Tonight, if I can just spend some time with her, things will start getting better. They have to.*

But now, as Jeff lay awake, the music still thumping incessantly, reality sunk in. *I'm losing Jenny. And maybe everything else.*

More Life Lessons—Kenny and Kristen

There were warm hugs and genuine expressions of affection as the friendly little gathering was breaking up.

"We love you guys!" said Kristen, as she offered a wide smile.

"You, too! Have a great night!" Tony and Tracy replied, more or less in unison.

As the couples retired to their neighboring homes, Kristen thought aloud, "Isn't it amazing how God can take a problem with a noisy old truck and turn it into a wonderful friendship?"

Kenny looked at her and laughed. "If God was able to take a guy like me and turn me into a decent husband, then it doesn't surprise me he can work miracles with a noisy old truck!"

Kristen took his hand and whispered coyly, "Hey, keep it down, Miracle Man—if we're quiet enough maybe we can get upstairs without waking the kids for a change."

With that Kenny whispered, "It's a deal" and began tiptoeing upstairs. Later, as Kenny was drifting off to peaceful sleep, with

Kristen snuggled up tightly in his arms, images of those first weeks with Tony and Tracy as neighbors started replaying in his mind like an old movie.

Tony and Tracy had just moved into the house next door. They looked very young and, like Kenny and Kristen, they had two very small children. It was early winter. Everything seemed fine at first, but then Tony began a very annoying late-night ritual.

Around 11:30 or so each night, Tony would go out and start up his rusty old truck, gunning the big engine repeatedly, literally causing the walls of Kenny and Kristen's house to shake. Finally, after about fifteen or twenty minutes of noisy idling, the rumbling old wreck would roar off loudly into the night. By this time, Kenny and Kristen's little ones would be awake and crying. It would be hours before things would settle back down.

After the third or fourth night of disruption, Kenny and Kristen were at the end of their ropes. As the engine rumbled, Kenny started getting dressed. "I've already talked to our neighbors across the street and down on the other side of Tony and Tracy," Kenny explained, "and they're all as annoyed as we are. I'm gonna go get 'em right now and we'll all go over and give our new neighbor a little lesson in courtesy."

Kristen was flustered, but had a brief flash of insight. "Kenny," she pleaded, "before you go out there tonight with those other guys, all pumped up and ready for a fight, let's please take some time and pray about this first."

Kenny reluctantly agreed and finally went back to bed. As they tried to fall back to sleep, they each asked God if there was something they should know, something they might be missing about this situation, something they needed to be sensitive to.

In the morning, Kenny suddenly remembered a Scripture verse, Matthew 18:15, in which Jesus taught about what to do if another person wronged you. "First, go to the other person privately was the basic point Jesus was making," Kenny explained to Kristen. "Last night, I almost messed that up."

Kristen shared that she had also remembered a biblical concept from Philippians 2:4: "God wants us to consider the needs of others as well as our own needs—especially because the person we're concerned about might not even be a Christian. The way we treat that person might ultimately lead them to find Christ or drive them farther away from him."

Kenny and Kristen quickly agreed that this situation with Tracy and Tony might be about much more than just a petty midnight inconvenience.

They decided that since they seldom saw Tracy outside, Kenny would try to go over and catch Tony when he came home from work that evening. And, instead of confronting him, Kristen would bake up a batch of cookies for Kenny to deliver. That way, maybe they could start talking a little and open the door to a more constructive discussion of the late-night noise problem.

Right away, Kenny knew they had made a wise decision. When he handed over the cookies, Tony smiled and exclaimed, "Tracy's gonna love these! With the new baby on the way, she's getting all kinds of cravings for sweets!" And then, hardly skipping a beat, Tony's expression turned very serious. "Hey, neighbor, by the way, I owe you an apology. I know my old truck makes a heck of a racket at night. Tracy's been working the midnight to 7 shift down at the truck stop—she gets double time. If she can hang in there for another month or so, we'll have enough saved up to buy a better set of wheels. And then she's quitting for good. I've been going out and getting the truck warmed up for her on these cold nights—in her condition I just don't think she should be sitting out in the cold and that heater ain't worth nothing until the engine gets good and hot."

Kenny was overwhelmed with appreciation for Kristen's counsel to pray before acting. He had almost gone out and verbally attacked a man who was only doing his best to take care of his pregnant wife. "Thank you, God," Kenny prayed silently.

As Kenny turned for home, something else hit him, a little spark of an idea, and he walked back to his neighbor's door. "Hey, Tony," he said, "I have something I want you to consider. My car has a good heater and it's a little more comfortable for a pregnant lady than that old beast of yours. Tracy gets back here by about 7:15 in the mornings, right?" Tony nodded cautiously. "Well, I don't leave for work until 7:30. How about if I give you a set of keys Tracy can use to drive my car to work until she's ready to quit? That way, you won't have to wake the neighborhood every night and your little princess can ride in style. If you'll promise to put some gas in it once in a while, I'll bring you my extra set of keys after supper tonight."

Tony stood there grinning. "Neighbor, you've got yourself a bargain!" he finally pronounced gleefully, locking onto Kenny's hand to seal the deal. Even now, years later, Kenny could still vividly remember the enthusiasm in Tony's voice and the powerful grip of that pumping handshake.

And as Kenny finally drifted off to sleep, reflecting peacefully, his last waking thoughts were of the day Tony and Tracy stood up and accepted Jesus at a church service he and Kristen had invited them to, and of the miracle of how their friendship had grown over the years to become a true bond of brotherhood and sisterhood in Christ.

Biblical Insights

Blessed are the peacemakers, for they will be called sons of God.
—Matthew 5:9

Settle matters quickly with your adversary who is taking you to court. Do it while you are still with him on the way, or he may hand you over to the judge, and the judge may hand you over to the officer, and you may be thrown into prison.—Matthew 5:25

And if someone wants to sue you and take your tunic, let him have your cloak as well. If someone forces you to go one mile, go with him two miles.—Matthew 5:40–41

Do not take revenge, my friends, but leave room for God's wrath, for it is written, "It is mine to avenge; I will repay," says the Lord. —Romans 12:19

If any of you has a dispute with another, dare he take it before the ungodly for judgment instead of before the saints? Do you not know that the saints will judge the world? And if you are to judge the world, are you not competent to judge trivial cases? Do you not know that we will judge angels? How much more the things of this life! Therefore, if you have disputes about such matters, appoint as judges even men of little account in the church! I say this to shame you. Is it possible that there is nobody among you wise enough to judge a dispute between believers? But instead, one brother goes to law against another—and this in front of unbelievers! The very fact that you have lawsuits among you means you have been completely defeated already. Why not rather be wronged? Why not rather be cheated?—1 Corinthians 6:1–7

"All things are lawful," but not all things are beneficial. "All things are lawful," but not all things build up. Do not seek your own advantage, but that of others.—1 Corinthians 10:23–24 (NRSV)

Make sure that nobody pays back wrong for wrong, but always try to be kind to each other and to everyone else.—1 Thessalonians 5:15

If your brother sins against you, go and show him his fault, just between the two of you. If he listens to you, you have won your brother over. But if he will not listen, take one or two others along, so that "every matter may be established by the testimony of two or three witnesses." If he refuses to listen to them, tell it to the church; and if he refuses to listen even to the church, treat him as you would a pagan or a tax collector.—Matthew 18:15–17

A man's wisdom gives him patience; it is to his glory to overlook an offense.—Proverbs 19:11

Practical Counsel

Imagine you're a golfer. You lose a golf ball in a patch of poison ivy. There's a big sign right there: DANGER—POISON IVY—KEEP OUT! YOU'LL BE TOTALLY MISERABLE IF YOU SET FOOT IN HERE! But it's a brand new ball you lost; and nobody tells *you* what to do. And it's just not fair that *your* ball is lost. And the whole principle of the thing just isn't right. So you go straight into the poison ivy patch, digging around, crawling around, until finally you come climbing out with your ball in hand, a little scratched and dirty, but you got your ball back. Now, in a day or so, you're going to wish you had never set foot anywhere near that poison ivy! You'll be so itchy and miserable that you would trade a million new golf balls just to be able to do it over again differently.

Do you think this illustration is absurd? Unrealistic? Well, that's the very sort of warning God has given us when it comes to litigation. If you read the Bible, you'll see that God has essentially posted a big sign in front of the courthouse: DANGER—POISON IVY—KEEP OUT!

Following God's biblical advice frees us from the kind of bondage and misery so often caused by typical secular attitudes toward disputes. How many times have you heard someone say, "Nobody takes advantage of me" or "I don't get mad, I get even"? That kind of thinking is so prevalent. And many secular attorneys just feed right into it, leading their clients down a path of grief and destruction. It appears some lawyers even play up their clients' emotions, as if they are trying to encourage lawsuits to gain more and more litigation business for themselves.

I've observed the emotional, physical, and economic toll that lawsuits and litigation can take on people. But Scripture teaches something totally different. Jesus Christ has a different plan for his children. He doesn't want us to be drawn into all that anguish and frustration. He has a different plan for us. He wants us to find joy and peace.

God strongly discourages Christians from being drawn into the trap of lawsuits and other litigation. A Christian empowered by God's Word is encouraged to step back and look at the big picture. And a person who dares to become the peacemaker in a hostile situation has a unique opportunity to experience the full blessing God has promised. As Christians, whenever we find ourselves embroiled in a conflict, even one in which we perceive we are the innocent party, before we do anything else, we need to first stop and pray, "God, can you show me how to become a peacemaker in the midst of this ugly mess?"

"Blessed are the peacemakers," Jesus said. That's such a hopeful statement for our world of ceaseless conflict and multiplying legal battles. But is it practical or just a pie-in-the-sky concept, some nice-sounding idealistic words? Thankfully, by the amazing work of God, Christian mediation and reconciliation are being rediscovered as legitimate alternatives to litigation and dispute (see chapter 13). As individual Christians, we can be actively working to bring about healing, resolution, and forgiveness in every situation we face. And for a watching world, every conflict turned into friendship and every dispute resolved amicably can become a powerful testimony of how Christ can take something Satan intends for evil and turn it around for good!

As a lawyer, I could profit financially by inflaming my clients' anger and stirring up their passion for immediate and satisfying revenge. But what would be the long-term result? More pain, more hurt, more misery for everyone involved. Instead, what if I encourage my clients to focus on an *eternal* perspective? If we really believe God is who he says he is, then we can leave it up to God to take care of any vengeance that might be required. After all, Scripture says that's his department, not ours. And meanwhile, we can help bring about healed hearts, reconciled relationships, and saved souls. We can help bring glory to Jesus Christ.

So, as Christians, what are we supposed to do if we're injured or hurt by someone else? How should we respond? Do we lash out and try to enforce all our "rights"? Do we seek to get "everything we deserve," like they promote in all those lawyers' commercials? Or do we respond by seeking reconciliation, as Jesus taught?

I believe that one of the hardest teachings in all Christianity is the notion of "turning the other cheek," the idea of "going the second mile" with someone who has done us wrong. We can read Christ's words about this in the gospels, we can understand them intellectually, but living them out when someone has hurt us is a different story. To me, it all comes down to the concept of grace.

Grace. We usually think of grace as a fancy church word, something theology professors might talk about. And yes, grace is a deep concept, with major theological implications, but it's also something very real that makes Christians different from the rest of the world. So how does grace fit in with reconciliation?

As Christian believers, we know that God sent his son, Jesus Christ, to die for us, so we, as condemned sinners, could be forgiven, set free, and reconciled to God. God did all that for us even though we don't deserve it, even though we really deserve punishment. So God responds to *our* mistakes (and even our intentional actions against him) not by asserting all his "rights" or by subjecting us to "everything we deserve." Instead, God gives us an incredible, undeserved gift of forgiveness. As Christians, shouldn't we do the same thing when other people make mistakes that hurt us? Aren't we in fact commanded to do so by Jesus Christ, whom we claim as Lord of our lives?

In the Lord's Prayer, Christ tells us we'll be forgiven as we forgive others. In one of his parables, Jesus taught about the king who forgave one of his servants, a servant who was in debt to the king so deeply he could *never* pay him back. The servant was extremely grateful to the king. But then the servant ran into a man who owed him a small amount of money. Instead of following the king's example of undeserved forgiveness, the servant treated the man very harshly, having him thrown in jail because he wouldn't repay. Well, when the king heard about that, he was, needless to say, terribly disappointed his servant didn't follow his example. It seems to me Christ told this story to encourage us to follow God's example of grace, extending forgiveness even to those who don't deserve it. As followers of Christ, instead of suing a person who hurts us, we must prayerfully consider forgiving the person instead, just as God has forgiven us.

So, to paraphrase a question posed in a typical lawyers' advertisement, "You're a Christian. You've been in a serious auto accident or hurt on the job. Now what?" The lawyers' ad would probably tell you to open the yellow pages and call a personal injury hotline to start your lawsuit. But is the yellow pages really the first place Christians should turn when they think they might have a legal claim? I have a much better idea. When we as Christians get hurt, are in an accident, or have any other reason to think we might have the "right" to sue someone else, let's not open the telephone book. Let's open *the* Book, God's Book, the Bible!

When you look through the attorneys' section in the yellow pages, what kind of words do you see? *Aggressive Representation. Get the Results You Deserve. Protect Your Rights. Enforce Your Rights.* Words that play to our egos, to our selfish desires to get the most for ourselves. But when you open the Bible, what kinds of words do you see? *Reconcile with your brother. Blessed are the peacemakers. Turn the other cheek. Go with him the second mile.* Exactly the opposite of what we see or hear in most lawyers' ads.

As Christians, we have to be alert and careful not to get caught up in the world's destructive ways. Lashing out at others to get all you can from them might feel satisfying at first, but it only leads to more pain and misery for everyone involved (including ourselves).

Now, I understand that many good, competent attorneys advertise in the yellow pages, and I'm not trying to criticize their skills or legal ethics. I'm just saying that the typical secular response of suing those who have hurt you is directly contrary to what Jesus taught. Jesus' words are all about reconciliation. The yellow pages advertisements are all about revenge.

Is there another way? An alternative to man's law, an alternative to the destructive human desire for revenge? Yes. The alternative is God's law. God's focus is on reconciling and restoring that which has been broken by sin. God's law encourages confession, forgiveness, and restoration of mutual respect. It's the opposite of humanity's revenge-driven system. Under God's law, the goal is *construction*, not *destruction*.

When it comes to lawsuits, the Bible does not portray a positive picture. In fact, God has essentially *nothing* good to say about lawsuits. In the Bible, God specifically tells us to keep out of lawsuits with other believers. Many Christians seem to be at least somewhat familiar with this idea. But many, many Christians seem to be genuinely surprised God also teaches us to keep out of lawsuits with nonbelievers. That doesn't leave us with much litigation, does it? As I've studied the issue, it has surprised me to learn how strongly God discourages Christians from becoming involved in litigation of any kind.

But why does God want us to keep out of lawsuits? Could it be he just doesn't like lawyers? After all, lawyers were always giving Jesus a hard time, trying to trip him up with trick questions and devious word traps. Jesus would have every reason to hate lawyers. It seems like everybody else does! But Jesus isn't the type to hold a grudge like that. So why *do* you think God wants Christians to stay out of lawsuits? We know how hurtful litigation can be for those involved, and obviously God does not want to see his children getting needlessly hurt, but is there something more? Is there some other reason God warns us to avoid lawsuits?

I suspect we can find the key in the concepts explained by the apostle Paul in the tenth chapter of 1 Corinthians. All things are lawful, Paul teaches, but not all things are beneficial. All things are lawful, Paul reminds us, but not all things build up (v. 23). And then, turning the world's wisdom upside down (and especially upsetting the prevailing wisdom in the secular legal arena), Paul challenges us not to seek our own advantage, but that of the other! (v. 24). Why? So, whether you eat or drink or whatever you do, Paul admonishes us, do everything for the glory of God! (v. 31). And to what end? Paul finally reveals his underlying purpose, his ultimate strategy: "Give no offense to Jews or Greeks or to the church of God, just as I try to please everyone in everything I do, not seeking my own advantage, but that of many, so that they may be saved" (vv. 32–33 NRSV). It's evangelism!

God wants us to take the focus off our own selfish concerns and put our focus where it belongs, on the salvation of souls. God knows lawsuits are almost always based on people seeking their own advantage, and he wants us to do just the opposite. God wants us to quit seeking our own advantage and start seeking to build up his kingdom. I think that's the deep, core reason God tells us to stay out of lawsuits and litigation, especially when nonbelievers are involved.

Having the local sheriff or constable serve someone with legal papers and then dragging that person before a judge and jury surely isn't the ideal way to show them Christ's love! God wants our focus to be on winning souls to Christ. Salvation and eternal judgment hang in the balance, and that's one verdict no courtroom judge or jury has the power to decide.

And how about when Christians sue fellow Christians? We've already alluded to the Christian perspective on lawsuits among believers. The Bible is very clear we Christians are not to sue one another in the secular courts. And it's in the form of a warning that when one of us takes another to court, all of us lose! That means the plaintiff loses, the defendant loses, and worst of all, the church of Jesus Christ loses in the eyes of an already skeptical world. Who's going to want to join a religion where members talk about loving each other but end up fighting each other in court? Litigation among believers is truly a "lose-lose" situation!

Am I saying it's a sin for a Christian to take someone to court? I don't remember there being an eleventh commandment: "You shall not sue." So it may not be an outright sin against God to file a lawsuit against someone, but it is clearly something God's Word does not recommend for us. I believe God's Word is the "owner's manual" for us as human beings. We might not always agree with or like what the Bible suggests, but God knows exactly what is good for us and what can hurt us, and when he tells us to avoid lawsuits, I take that very seriously.

In the fictional illustrations I've shared at the beginning of this chapter, the scenarios might be considered by some as being rather trivial. Perhaps, a reader might ask, I can forgive my neighbor for making excessive noise, but what if a close family member has been severely injured or even killed as a result of someone else's negligence? Then what? It is indeed a sobering situation, one in which the aggrieved persons will need to seek much prayerful counsel and support. But I have found nothing in God's Word to limit his teachings on litigation to trivial matters only. I am forced to conclude that God desires us to avoid litigation over even the most serious offenses.

As Christians, we can be proactive in living out God's teaching on lawsuits and other litigation, seeing the big picture from a Christian perspective, and choosing to avoid subjecting ourselves and others to the grief, anxiety, and frustration that accompanies almost every court case. I've practiced law for many years, yet I can't recall a plaintiff or a defendant having fun or talking about what a great experience litigation has been, or a nonbeliever professing Jesus Christ as Lord and Savior as a result of a lawsuit.

CHAPTER 2

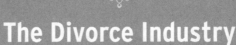

The Divorce Industry

"I hate divorce," says the Lord God of Israel.

—MALACHI 2:16

Life Lessons—Rick and Rachel

Rachel was surprised how easy it was to hold back the tears as the rented truck rolled out of the driveway and down the street, with Rick at the wheel and his share of their belongings in the back. And the girls really did seem to understand. Sure, some things would change, but they'd still have a mom and a dad. And she got to keep the house, so they'd be in a familiar place at least half the time. *Life is hard,* she thought to herself. *It always has been and it always will be. It's probably good for them in the long run, so they don't expect things in life to come too easy.*

And sure, Rachel remembered seeing some of the statistics a speaker at her mother-in-law's—or, she caught herself, her *ex-*mother-in-law's church—had passed around, the stuff about how girls growing up without a dad at home were so much more likely to engage in all kinds of risky behaviors as teenagers. But she was certain her girls would be okay and she'd always keep a close eye on them.

"Now," she mumbled absentmindedly, "whom can I get to watch the girls after school tomorrow while I'm out job hunting?"

The phone rang. "Yes, Mr. Gordon," Rachel said matter-of-factly, "that's right. We'll be pulling the girls out of the Christian school at the end of the month. With the divorce and everything, keeping two separate households, we just won't be able to afford the tuition. Thanks for all your help with the paperwork."

Rachel was actually relieved. Rick was always the one insisting the girls should be at the Christian school, always the one going on and on about how vital it was to pass the faith down to the next generation, always making such a big deal about it. Rachel wasn't so sure and she never quite understood why it was so important to Rick, and why he was always asking her whether she was really at peace with God, whether she considered herself "born-again." She shook her head slowly, thinking, *What difference does it make anyway? I believe in God—isn't that enough? It'll be good for the girls to get out in the real world, away from all those fanatics at that school. If the rest of them are anything like Rick, they're nothing but hypocrites.*

Now Rachel gritted her teeth with anger as her thoughts drifted further. *How could Rick have betrayed me like that? That's one thing I will* never *get over. I will* never *forgive that man. Nobody cheats on me and gets away with it.* She remembered the day he had first confessed to her about the whole thing, his story about the business trip, the late-night meeting, how somehow things just got out of control. And she remembered how he tearfully begged for forgiveness and promised over and over it would never happen again. *Thank God I had the sense to call Janie Jones before I fell for any of Rick's lines,* she reflected with cold satisfaction.

Janie Jones was a local attorney specializing in divorce cases, usually representing wives. She prided herself on her toughness and pragmatism. She was a realist, she told herself, and because of that, she could make sure her clients got exactly what they deserved. Rachel had recently struck up a casual friendship with Janie while working out at the health club.

The first thing Janie told Rachel when she called the law office was to get over any illusions about saving the marriage. "Rachel, I've seen so many of these cases it would make your head spin. There's always more going on than what he tells you. I'll start doing some digging. The reality is, the faster we act, the more legal advantages we'll have. You'll never be able to trust him again, Rachel. The sooner you accept the fact the marriage is over, the sooner you'll be able to get on with your life. The divorce process is really not that difficult. I deal with this stuff every day and I'll take good care of you. You deserve better than Rick. And he doesn't deserve you after what he's done. Just don't make a move from here on out without checking with me first."

Rachel had felt such a rush of power in talking to Janie that first time. And she could tell Janie really sympathized with her, really understood her anger at Rick. With Janie's help, things moved swiftly. They quickly maneuvered Rick into voluntarily moving to his parents' house for a "temporary separation." When Rick suggested attending joint marriage counseling with a Christian counselor their pastor recommended, Janie quickly nixed the idea. "Rachel, I have a guy we always use. He'll get you through the mandatory sessions and make just the kind of assessment we need to support our case. Trust me, we don't want to mess this up by involving some off-the-wall religious kook."

And now, just like Janie promised, it was all over. As she stood alone in the living room, Rachel could hear one of the girls coughing upstairs. *Oh, no,* she fretted, *she'd better not be getting sick. I won't be able to start looking for a job tomorrow if she's home from school all day.* The phone rang again, interrupting her worry. It was one of Rachel's girlfriends, calling to invite her on a ladies-only shopping outing that Saturday. "I'll see if I can get a sitter for the girls," she replied, forcing a cheerful tone as she secretly wondered where she could find a sitter and how much money she had left in her dwindling checking account.

When Rachel entered the kitchen to start cooking dinner, her feet splashed in an unexpected and rapidly growing puddle of water on the floor, water flowing from somewhere under the sink. Instinctively, she started to shout, "Rick! There's . . ." But as the words echoed emptily, something cold suddenly gripped her heart. Another flood began in her mind, memories welling up uncontrollably: the night of their engagement, their wedding day, the births of the girls, the closeness they had shared, smiling faces, laughter, everything was there. Waves of sorrow overwhelmed her and she began to weep. Suddenly it was all beginning to sink in. She was on her own now. Rick was gone. Janie Jones wasn't there to direct her every move. She was alone. "Oh, Lord," she gasped, "what have I done?"

More Life Lessons—Manuel and Maria

Manuel called his lawyer nervously, not sure what to say first. When attorney Cliff Calaman finally came on the line, Manuel cleared his throat. "Cliff, this is the most difficult phone call I've ever had to make. I found out this weekend that Maria has been unfaithful to me. Cliff, I'm calling you because I know you're a Christian lawyer. Doesn't the Bible say adultery is proper grounds for divorce?"

Cliff paused for a long moment. "Listen, Manny," Cliff finally began, "I've known you for a long time, and I know how much you've always loved Maria. Let's slow down for a few minutes here before we start throwing around the 'D-word,' okay?"

Manuel started speaking more rapidly now. "Cliff, you don't understand some things. It was a guy from down at the plant where I work. Everyone else seems to know about it. I look like a fool. Not only can't I forgive Maria, but I have to protect my reputation as well. How's it gonna look if I just let her get away with it? Cliff, I'm no weakling and I will not be taken advantage of!"

Cliff had begun to pray silently for the assistance of the Holy Spirit as soon as Manuel had mentioned the word *divorce*. Now he seized on something he thought he had heard Manuel say.

"Manny, you mentioned you can't forgive Maria. Does that mean she has asked you for forgiveness?"

Manuel stammered, "Yes, that's how I finally found out about the whole thing. She came to me Saturday night and confessed, and then she begged for forgiveness. She said it was all a terrible mistake, that she loves me now more than ever. But Cliff, that's more than a man can take. I flew off the handle and told her our marriage is over."

"Look, Manny," Cliff replied, now gaining confidence, "I can see why you're so upset and, quite frankly, as a Christian I do believe the Bible teaches that marital unfaithfulness is a legitimate grounds for divorce. If need be, I would even agree to represent you in a divorce proceeding against Maria. But honestly, brother to brother, I don't believe that what you face is a legal problem."

Now Manuel was becoming curious. "What are you talking about, Cliff?" he asked.

Cliff continued, "Manny, I know you're a tough guy, and I know that your pride has been hurt. But I know you're a Christian. And what I want to know, Manny, is this: Are you man enough to try to save your marriage?"

Manuel was not sure whether to be annoyed or appreciative of Cliff's challenge. He had called his lawyer to get help in ending his marriage and now the guy was trying to make him save it. But the bottom line was simple. He could never trust Maria again and he would never forgive her. After a brief silence, Manuel responded firmly, "It's not possible, Cliff. This marriage is dead."

But Manuel was not prepared when Cliff replied, "Well, that's perfect, Manny, because Jesus Christ is in the resurrection business." And then he proposed a deal: "Manny, as I said, I will agree to represent you in the divorce, but only on one condition. There's a Christian marriage counselor I know. She counsels from biblical principles and, with the Lord's help, I have seen her work miracles. If you will go with Maria for a month of counseling sessions with this Christian counselor, then, if you still need me, I'll be here to handle your divorce."

Manny had been reluctant to accept Cliff's challenge. Finally, that evening as he prayed, his heart softened just enough to agree to try the counseling, although he was convinced it would never help. That was more than two months ago now. Manny and Maria had worked through some very difficult days. Often, he found himself deeply discouraged, sometimes losing hope altogether. And no matter what happened, there would always be scars.

But, Manuel had to admit, something new was beginning to happen. Despite his intentions, he could feel his love for Maria rekindling deep inside. As he studied some Scripture passages the marriage counselor had recommended, he began to truly ponder what it could possibly mean for him to love his wife "as Christ loved the church."

And then one day, it happened. The burden lifted from his heart. And when he spoke the words to her that evening, "Maria, I forgive you," it was a moment like neither of them had ever experienced.

"Praise God, praise God, praise God," was all Maria was able to say through her tears.

So when Manuel called his friend Cliff this time, things were quite different from two months before. At first, Cliff was cautious, not knowing what to expect. But something in Manuel's tone of voice quickly told him the news would be good. "Cliff, I can never explain how much what you did means to Maria and me," Manuel said appreciatively. "We're sending you a gift certificate for dinner at the Olde Inn, so you and Connie can enjoy a nice evening together, but really that's just a token. What you did for us is priceless and only God has the power to reward you properly."

Cliff responded gratefully, and then added, "It's good to have a friend in the resurrection business."

Biblical Insights

Some Pharisees came and tested [Jesus] by asking, "Is it lawful for a man to divorce his wife?" "What did Moses command you?" he replied. They said, "Moses permitted a man to write a certificate of divorce and send her away." "It was because your hearts were hard that Moses wrote you this law," Jesus replied. "But at the beginning of creation God 'made them male and female.' 'For this reason a man will leave his father and mother and be united to his wife, and the two will become one flesh.' So they are no longer two, but one. Therefore what God has joined together, let man not separate." When they were in the house again, the disciples asked Jesus about this. He answered, "Anyone who divorces his wife and marries another woman commits adultery against her. And if she divorces her husband and marries another man, she commits adultery."—Mark 10:2–12

To the married I give this command (not I, but the Lord). A wife must not separate from her husband. But if she does, she must remain unmarried or else be reconciled to her husband. And a husband must not divorce his wife.—1 Corinthians 7:10–12

It has been said, "Anyone who divorces his wife must give her a certificate of divorce." But I tell you that anyone who divorces his wife, except for marital unfaithfulness, causes her to become an adulteress, and anyone who marries the divorced woman commits adultery. —Matthew 5:31–32

Jesus looked at them and said, "With man this is impossible, but not with God; all things are possible with God."—Mark 10:27

Husbands, in the same way be considerate as you live with your wives, and treat them with respect as the weaker partner and as heirs with you of the gracious gift of life, so that nothing will hinder your prayers.—1 Peter 3:7

Practical Counsel

The Scriptures tell us God hates divorce. And, as Christians, we know that true joy is found in doing what is right before God, living according to his will. So I don't believe that God intends for Christians to simply endure bad marriage relationships and be miserable. Instead I believe that God has a vision of healing for *every* marriage, a plan to restore marriage into the incredible blessing he designed it to be, for both husbands and wives.

Marriage is a covenant relationship established before God. Divorce is the destruction of that covenant. Divorce has a devastating and far-reaching impact on the lives of those directly involved and even on the rest of us, who aren't so directly involved. We all pay a heavy price for divorce. The pain from a divorce radiates out into the community surrounding the divorcing couple like waves from a rock tossed into a pond, disrupting and disturbing friendships and family relationships, sometimes even other marriages.

I don't keep official statistics, but sometimes it seems like almost every week I get at least one call at the office from someone looking for legal help with a divorce. And Christians seem to be having as much trouble holding their marriages together as anyone else. I've even read some statistics claiming the divorce rate is actually higher among Christians than among non-Christians. It's almost as if we Christians are being cut off from the sound biblical counsel that might help us avoid the big, painful legal mess we call divorce.

As Christian spouses, are we demonstrating by our actions that our life together with our husband or wife is the top priority for us, after our relationship with God himself? Can you imagine what a positive impact it would have on the strength of marriages in our society if every Christian spouse would take God's Word and put it into action in his or her marriage? Can you imagine the number of marriages that might be saved if every divorce lawyer would begin domestic-relations client consultations with a careful Bible study on what it means for a husband or wife to honor his or her spouse? Maybe I would finally stop getting all those sad divorce calls.

God's Word contains the power to save marriages, if Christian spouses are willing to find the courage to take its example to heart. That's the challenge for Christian spouses when our marriages are in trouble. As believers in Christ, are we willing to step into the breach for him? Are we willing to do what's right in the eyes of God? Our society, our neighborhoods, our churches, our families, and our marriages stand on the edge of destruction. But we don't have to let them be destroyed, and we certainly don't have to accelerate the process of destruction by employing divorce lawyers who don't share our hope in Christ or our faith in God's power to heal damaged marriages.

If you're reading this in the midst of marital problems or even a pending divorce, I challenge you to ask God for help and step faithfully into the breach to give all you have in order to save yourself and others from the pain and destruction of a dissolved marriage covenant. It's not too late. God is ready. I pray that this might be a word of conviction for you, a word received with humility and an open heart.

If you're a parent in the middle of a divorce or custody battle, I especially pray that you would be willing to stand in the breach for your own children. Don't make those kids pawns in your chess match against your estranged spouse. Don't fill those kids with disrespect toward their other parent. Don't drag those kids through the dark valley of your own anger and resentment. Parents, if ever there's a place where kids are going to see whether your faith is the real thing or just a lot of empty talk, it's going to be in the way you handle yourself in a serious conflict with their other parent. Are you conducting yourself in a Christlike way? Will God be proud of the way you're stepping into the gap to save your marriage and family?

In my experience, next to prayerfully seeking God and opening his Word, the most essential step for any Christian facing a marital crisis is getting connected with a solid source of Christian counseling. It might be a well-trained pastor or someone else from your church trained in biblical marriage counseling, or it might be an independent Christian counseling agency. The most important thing is for the counselor to be thoroughly versed in and genuinely committed to a biblical, Christ-centered approach. Without Christ, any so-called "marriage counselor" will be relying merely on the weakness of worldly wisdom to save your marriage. Without Christ, the odds will be stacked against you from the start. But when Christ is put at the center, marriage counseling can become a saving blessing for marriages in trouble.

Tragically, instead of referring clients to Christian counseling in the hope of healing marriages, many divorce lawyers (including many so-called "Christian divorce lawyers") are more than willing to jump right into the fray and start fanning the flames of disaster. The Scriptures teach "If anyone teaches false doctrines and does not agree to the sound instruction of our Lord Jesus Christ and to godly teaching, he is conceited and understands nothing. He has an unhealthy interest in controversies and quarrels about words that result in envy, strife, malicious talk, evil suspicions, and constant friction between men of corrupt mind, who have been robbed of the truth and who think that godliness is a means to financial gain" (1 Timothy 6:3–5).

Far too many lawyers, even Christian lawyers, choose to act like nothing more than overly enthusiastic cheerleaders for their clients. We've all seen how cheerleaders stand on the sidelines at a game, smiling, celebrating, and cheering, even while their team is getting deeper and deeper into a hole. Well, if I'm doing something wrong or destructive to others, or myself, the last thing I want is a cheerleader cheering my every move. What I want is a coach, someone who can tell it like it really is and teach me to move beyond my mistakes to real victory. A coach who might even pull me out of the game and make me sit on the bench if my bad attitude is getting in the way of my team's success (or my family's success, in this case).

In the field of family law more than any other, Christian lawyers should be coaches for our clients, not cheerleaders who cheer them down the path to unnecessary controversy and dissension and destroyed relationships. An attorney's zealous representation of his or her client's best interests is not to be confused with catering to the client's every foolish whim and hurtful desire. Sometimes the best advocate will be the one who dares to challenge a client to move beyond the petty impulses arising from a broken marriage relationship to look instead at the bigger picture, to move from the goal of revenge to the goal of reconciliation and restoration.

In this chapter on divorce and marriage, I must acknowledge the sad reality that some marriages—even some marriages among Christians—are threatened by more than typical demons such as poor communication, lack of attention, or outside temptations. Sometimes the threat comes from physical violence or abuse inflicted by one spouse upon the other, or even upon the children or extended family members. In such a situation, I would not hesitate to advise the "at-risk" spouse to take immediate measures to protect her physical well-being (and that of her children). These measures might include seeking shelter at a domestic-violence safe house, seeking godly counsel from spiritually mature and qualified individuals, and even consulting with an experienced attorney with respect to applicable civil and criminal proceedings aimed at protection of life and limb. The prevailing heart attitude should still remain one of hope for repentance, restoration, and forgiveness, as should be the goal of any legal proceedings. But the reality of the situation might dictate the need for chaperoned counseling sessions and restricted or supervised visitation, and the road to restoration and healing may be long and treacherous, though God's ability to work miracles even in the deepest and darkest of places must not be discounted.

CHAPTER 3

The Prenuptial Blues

For this reason a man will leave his father and mother
and be united to his wife, and they will become one flesh.

—GENESIS 2:24

Life Lessons—Tim and Tiffany

"Everything's set, Mom!" chirped Tiffany. She was so excited she couldn't sit still. That morning she had tried on the gown. She could tell right away Tim was going to love it—or rather, he was going to love her in it—and she could barely wait for him to see her. Now as she bounced around the apartment chatting with her mother on the phone, it all seemed like a fairy tale. By this time on Saturday, she would actually be married to her handsome prince!

It still amazed Tiffany that a guy like Tim would be interested in a girl like her. She'd had a hard life growing up and went to work right out of high school. A couple of years later she landed a job waitressing in an upscale hotel dining room. The tips were good and after a few months she was even able to afford her own little two-room rental place. But Tim was from a different world altogether. He was a recent college graduate, from one of those expensive schools. While Tim was interning with one of the downtown banks, he would stop in to eat lunch at the hotel.

There was no way to explain it except "love at first sight." The moment Tiffany brought the water glasses to Tim's table, there was an instant connection. "Chemistry" is what Tim called it. Whatever it was, she liked it, and now her dreams were coming true! Tim even wanted to have a big family someday and promised Tiffany he would take care of her so she could stay at home and be an old-fashioned mom to their kids. It was all like a dream.

As soon as Tiffany hung up from talking with her mother, the phone rang again. She answered cheerfully to an unfamiliar woman's voice. "Ms. Tyson? Is this Tiffany Tyson?" When Tiffany acknowledged her identity, the caller continued, sounding very formal, "I'm calling from the law firm of Cummings and Cantwell in Chicago. I have the prenuptial agreement ready for your signature. Of course, it's imperative that you thoroughly review the agreement with your own legal counsel before you sign it. Can you provide me with your attorney's name and number, in order that I might make arrangements to send it over? And, of course, the agreement must be finalized and signed before Saturday."

Tiffany was puzzled and asked the caller if she could explain what she was talking about. Sounding a bit annoyed now, the caller went on, "Ms. Tyson, let me make myself more clear. You're planning to marry Tim Torrington on Saturday. Mr. Torrington and his family have some concerns about this wedding—or, rather, some issues regarding this marriage—that they feel should be addressed. On behalf of Mr. Torrington, our firm has been engaged to prepare an agreement with provisions appropriate to protect his interests."

Tiffany was trembling now, confused, replaying those ominous-sounding and unexpected words—"concerns" and "issues"—

over and over in her head. "I'm sorry," she finally said abruptly, "you'll have to call back."

Within minutes, she had reached Tim. She had so many questions. What "concerns" did Tim and his family have about her? What were the "issues"? Wasn't she good enough, or rich enough, for them? Why hadn't Tim mentioned any of this before?

Tim stammered and struggled to answer her barrage of questions. "A prenuptial agreement is just a normal part of sensible planning for any couple," he explained. "It has nothing to do with you or who you are."

Still, to Tiffany, something about his answers sounded evasive—something just wasn't right. "Tim," she finally said slowly, "is there anything else you didn't tell me about?"

"No, of course not, Tiff," he replied nonchalantly. Suddenly she didn't know whether to believe him.

And now, with her heart beginning to pound, she asked him one more question. "Tim, what happens if I don't sign that agreement?"

There was a long pause, and Tim finally answered, as if reluctant, "Tiffany, if you don't sign the agreement, then the wedding will have to be delayed."

Resisting every impulse in her body to cry, Tiffany managed to form the final words she needed to say. "Then forget it, Tim. The wedding's off!" And throwing the phone down hard against the floor, she broke into tears.

More Life Lessons—Ben and Brooke

Brooke was so anxious about meeting Ben's parents. Here it was, the week of her wedding and she was meeting her in-laws-to-be for the very first time. Ben was the light of her life and she wanted so badly to make a good impression on his folks. He always spoke so highly of them, and always told Brooke he wanted to have a marriage just like theirs.

At the airport, Ben quickly spotted his parents at a distance as they disembarked after the long flight from the East Coast. Brooke intently watched Mr. and Mrs. Bradford shuffling through the gate area with the other passengers, looking a little bewildered. The first thing Brooke noticed was that they were holding hands. *Wow,* she thought, *there really must be some magic there!*

The Bradfords' eyes lit up as soon as they saw Ben, and they greeted both Ben and Brooke with warm hugs, immediately insisting that Brooke call them "Mom" and "Dad." "I can live with that," she chuckled, feeling an almost tangible sense of unconditional acceptance.

The two couples made plans for a dinner out later that evening, after the Bradfords had a chance to get some rest at the hotel. When they finally all gathered around the table at a quiet restaurant, the Bradfords started with an announcement, advising Brooke they had some things they would like to share with her. She thought it all seemed rather official sounding, but she optimistically assented.

Mrs. Bradford began, "From the moment of the wedding on, Brooke, we will consider you to be our daughter, no matter what might happen in the future." Brooke glanced quickly at Ben, her smile widening, and gave his hand a tighter squeeze.

"So you might as well get used to us!" quipped Mr. Bradford jovially.

"I think that's going to be very easy!" Brooke shot back, already feeling at ease in this new family.

"But even more important than our relationship with you, Brooke, is your relationship with Ben," Mrs. Bradford picked up. "My husband and I have been blessed with twenty-six wonderful years together, and we can both honestly say we love each other more today than we did even on our wedding day. As you and Ben prepare for your own wedding day, we wanted to pass along to you the secret of our success."

As Mr. Bradford nodded, his wife continued, "Early on, we learned that God's Word, the Bible, describes his plan for marriage as a man and woman becoming 'one flesh.' Now some Christians might think this refers primarily to the physical relationship between a husband and wife—and that's certainly something that's been important in our relationship, something we both treasure . . ."

At this, Ben hurriedly interrupted his mother. "Don't you think it's time we place our orders, everyone? It's already late."

But Mrs. Bradford would have none of that. "Ben, I won't go into any more details and I'm not trying to embarrass you, but we do want to pass along to you and Brooke as many of the blessings of marriage as we can."

Mr. Bradford nodded his head and, winking at his wife, said, "Amen."

As they all laughed, Mrs. Bradford again picked up, "Now, as I was saying, there is more to becoming one flesh than physical intimacy alone. There is also a oneness of soul and spirit that comes from sharing as much of life as you can with each other. For us, that has meant things as simple as keeping all our financial dealings combined, to things as difficult as giving up activities and even friendships we realized were diminishing our own relationship. What I'm really saying is that from the moment you both say 'I do,' you each become the number one thing in each other's lives, next to God Almighty himself. It won't always be easy, but let me promise you this: You will never regret treating your marriage as a sacred gift from God."

As soon as Mrs. Bradford finished her speech, Brooke spoke up enthusiastically, "Mrs. Brad—I mean Mom—thank you so much for sharing that with Ben and me! You know, my parents were divorced when I was young and I never really got to see what a good, healthy marriage is supposed to look like. And you know, I'm kind of new at this whole Christianity thing, too. All I can say is that now that I've met you and Mr.—I mean now that I've met you and Dad—I can see why I love Ben so much!"

Mrs. Bradford, now flushed by the compliment, reached her hand across the table to touch Brooke's and said reassuringly, "Brooke, if there's ever anything I can do for you, if there's ever any question I can help you answer, you call me, alright? And one more thing. Brooke and Ben, your Dad and I have made a covenant with each other to pray often for the strength of your new marriage, so please rest in confidence in God and in that foundation of prayer. Okay, kids?"

Biblical Insights

For this reason a man will leave his father and mother and be united to his wife, and they will become one flesh.—Genesis 2:24

Practical Counsel

The words from the book of Genesis are familiar to many Christians: "For this reason a man will leave his father and mother and be united to his wife, and they will become one flesh." Likewise, many Christians are familiar with the concept of "prenuptial agreements."

Basically, a prenuptial agreement is a legal contract entered into by a man and woman before they get married. Usually it spells out what happens if they later get divorced, who gets what, all the legal details and arrangements. A prenuptial agreement is utilized for essentially the same reason people generally make a written agreement when entering into a new business relationship: to "protect yourself going in," so there won't be any unpleasant surprises if things unravel, and to "get it in writing."

With so many marriages ending in divorce, more and more engaged couples are seriously considering whether they should have a prenuptial agreement. And many times their parents or other relatives are even encouraging and promoting the idea.

But let me ask you a question: Suppose that a few weeks before your wedding date your future spouse unexpectedly handed you a fifteen-page prenuptial agreement and told you to go hire a lawyer to look it over with you? How would you feel? (Many people reading this book may have been through this very experience.) Would you feel disappointed? Mistrusted? Insulted?

I think that's precisely the problem with prenuptial agreements, even in those cases where both spouses like the idea at first. The very nature of the prenuptial agreement puts the husband and wife in an adversarial relationship, starting before the wedding rings are exchanged. It sets the foundation of the marriage on a lack of mutual trust. And how much easier will it be for the couple to give up on the whole marriage when they run into the inevitable rough spot or two if the escape route is already spelled out in black and white?

This is why I believe Christians need to think long and hard before they consider entering into a prenuptial agreement. Think about what God means in Genesis when he talks about the two being united as one flesh. How can you be unified as one when you have a legal document keeping you separate? This is one time when I, as an attorney, recommend *less* paperwork!

How committed to each other should a Christian husband and wife be? Should they be 50 percent committed? Seventy percent committed? Is a 90 percent commitment enough?

Isn't the answer 100 percent? When God teaches us about marriage, when he uses those words "one flesh," it sounds to me like God intends for husbands and wives to be 100 percent committed to each other. But the existence of a prenuptial agreement sets the husband and wife at odds with each other. It's like saying, "Honey, let's agree up front that we aren't necessarily 100 percent committed to each other." As a Christian attorney, I am very reluctant to endorse the use of prenuptial agreements. To me, they just don't seem consistent with God's design for Christian marriage.

Despite my reservations, many people would argue that under certain conditions a prenuptial agreement is essential, even for a Christian couple. An example might be when one spouse brings much more material wealth into the marriage than the other. Another example might be when it's a second marriage and children from previous marriages are involved. The arguments used can sound very persuasive.

The world aggressively pushes the notion that it would be foolish not to have a prenuptial agreement in these and certain other circumstances. But let's go back to Genesis and God's plan for marriage, for husband and wife to become "one flesh." Did God put an exception in Scripture for second marriages? Was there a special footnote for marriages where one spouse was much wealthier than the other? No! God said, "One flesh!"

Lawyers could probably think up a thousand different situations where cold logic and a secular perspective might dictate that the spouses "need" a prenuptial agreement. But under God's plan, what either spouse has "going in" doesn't really matter because everything belongs *fully* to both spouses once they're married. If either spouse feels they can't freely give everything to the other, then, quite frankly, I would suggest they reconsider going through with the marriage.

Please understand I am not advising that the couple should do no planning, especially if there are minor children or children with special needs involved. Those scenarios can and should be provided for by the couple through joint planning and discussion with qualified counsel, but in a voluntary manner, within the context of a wholehearted commitment to the marriage. And when husband and wife choose to make their relationship with each other the highest priority next to their own relationships with Christ, it sets an example for the next generation much more powerful than any financial legacy they could ever leave. And as for adult children who fear that "their" inheritance may end up in the hands of step-mom or stepdad, I would humbly suggest that those children need to examine their own hearts to determine why they are elevating personal financial considerations over the quality and richness of their parent's new marriage.

It might sound old-fashioned, or even foolish, but when Christians choose to marry, they are signing up for a lifetime commitment. Neither spouse should be planning to give the marriage anything less than all they have. To me, setting up a prenuptial agreement creates an environment in which the spouses are encouraged to hold something back from each other. And I see that as a recipe for disaster.

CHAPTER 4

The Criminal-Defense Dilemma

Now if I am in the wrong and have committed something for
which I deserve to die, I am not trying to escape death; but if
there is nothing to their charges against me, no one can
turn me over to them. I appeal to the emperor.

—ACTS 25:11 (NRSV)

Life Lessons—Ralph

It had been a long, stressful day at the real estate agency. Deals going
sour, angry phone calls—the whole nine yards. When Ralph finally
got on the interstate, he was already running twenty minutes late
for his Monday night golf league. He was in the far left lane passing a line of trucks when he saw the red lights in the rearview mir-
ror. *No way,* he muttered to himself in disbelief, *no way.* But it was
true. Before he knew it, there he was, pulled over on the shoulder
handing his license and registration to the stern young state trooper.

As Ralph sat waiting for the trooper to run driver's license and
license plate numbers through the patrol car's computer, his mind

was already thinking about the argument he had just lost. *It's totally unfair,* he consoled himself. *There's no way I could have seen those construction-zone signs along the right shoulder through all those trucks. I didn't think the construction was for another half mile. And the only reason that cocky young kid stopped me was because of the construction-zone speed limit. I blow through here doing 75 or 80 all the time and no cop ever stopped me before, but now that there's a temporary construction-zone speed limit of 55 instead of 65, they nailed me just to collect the big fine. And I wasn't the only one in the left lane either—what about the cars in front of me? I'm gonna fight this,* Ralph whispered to himself. *I'll show that snotty young punk he picked the wrong guy to lay a bogus ticket on this time.*

When Ralph finally got home from the golf course late that night, the first thing he did was grab the telephone book. He opened it to "Attorneys" and right away a big ad for a lawyer specializing in defending traffic citation cases caught his eye, the words "Not Guilty" highlighted in big red letters. He circled the ad and made a plan to call the lawyer in the morning, still indignant over the whole incident.

The next day he set his appointment and spent most of the afternoon traveling to the nearby town where the lawyer's office was, meeting with him to discuss the case, and then making his way back to the agency through heavy late-day traffic. The lawyer basically told Ralph his case wasn't the strongest he had ever seen, but that there was always a chance to beat the ticket on a technicality or if the trooper didn't show up in court to testify. Ralph was frustrated the lawyer wasn't more sympathetic to his story, but he paid the required retainer and waited for his day in court. A few weeks later all the paperwork was filed and a court date was set: June 16, 3:30 p.m. Back at the real estate agency, Ralph bragged to his associates, "In this country, a man is innocent until proved guilty, and they aren't gonna pin this ticket on me without a fight."

Finally, the big day came. June 16. The trooper showed up. He had done everything by the book. Ralph got to explain his story. When he was finished, the judge quickly announced, "Guilty as charged." Ralph spoke out in protest, raising his voice, but the lawyer quickly intervened, escorting him from the courtroom and handing him a final bill.

Ralph was seething. When he finally got home that evening, he flipped on the local TV news. There was a report about a violent incident a few hours earlier that day, out on the interstate in a construction zone. A minor accident had led to heated words between two motorists. Things escalated until one of the motorists pulled a gun. The other was now in critical condition in the local trauma unit with a gunshot wound. The shooter was still at large. *Where're the cops when you need 'em?* thought Ralph angrily to himself. *Too busy chasing guys like me to protect people from the real criminals.* Nothing registered with Ralph as the TV reporter on the scene mentioned the time of the incident. "The shooting occurred at approximately 3:30 this afternoon," she said, "and despite a large number of witnesses, there were apparently no police officers in the area at that time."

More Life Lessons—Victor

"Victor! Look out, Vic!"

As his brother's voice rang out, Victor hit the brakes hard and the tires squealed. He could see the panic in the eyes of the highway department worker as the car lurched to a halt just inches in front of her. Instantly, Victor began to sweat. His hands started to tremble. His brother, Tommaso, was already out of the car checking on the frightened woman.

Victor felt frozen in place behind the wheel and didn't even notice the police officer approaching his window until he heard him rapping on the glass with his flashlight. Victor finally managed to open the window only to hear a familiar voice.

"Victor Velasquez, well, well, well . . . we meet again."

Victor looked up into the face of Officer Blackstone of the city police department. The same officer who had ticketed Victor for speeding in a construction zone just two days before. "Some of us are slow learners," Officer Blackstone said wryly.

Victor's normal impulse would have been to argue, to take the bait and jump down the officer's throat with words of his own. But something had suddenly changed. All Victor could manage was a weak "Yes. I'm sorry, officer. I nearly killed her."

Officer Blackstone could see the look on Victor's face and he knew instantly this was no act. "Look, Victor," the officer stated, "I could write this up a couple of different ways. I could cite you for half-a-dozen violations and you'd probably lose your license. But I have a feeling you won't be speeding in any work zones anytime soon. I'm just gonna cite you for the speeding violation and we'll let it go at that."

Again Victor answered in a way that surprised even himself: "Thank you, Officer. I deserve much worse."

By this time, Tommaso had returned to the car and looked at his brother incredulously. When Officer Blackstone finally walked away, Tommaso started in, "What are you talking about, man!? It was that stupid woman's fault for wandering out in traffic. You can fight this. She was the one who was negligent—either that or just plain dumb. I'm your witness. And that cop, he didn't even have his radar gun out, so how can he prove you were speeding?"

Victor responded in slow measured tones, "Tommaso, I know what I've been like in the past, but something happened to me just now. God saved me from the consequences of the biggest mistake I ever made in my life. I thought this whole speeding thing was just a game. But today I almost killed an innocent woman. God has been merciful to me. I deserve whatever punishment I get. I don't care if they throw me in jail. I deserve it. I just thank God he helped me stop this car before it was too late."

Tommaso protested, "But what about the fine? What about your insurance? You've got to fight it, man!"

Victor looked his brother in the eye. "No, Tommaso. I have to accept the consequences. Let's go find a church somewhere. I need to do some serious praying."

Biblical Insights

He who conceals his sins does not prosper, but whoever confesses and renounces them finds mercy.—Proverbs 28:13

No one brings suit justly, no one goes to law honestly; they rely on empty pleas, they speak lies, conceiving mischief and begetting iniquity . . . Therefore justice is far from us, and righteousness does not reach us; we wait for light, and lo! there is darkness; and for brightness, but we walk in gloom . . . Justice is turned back, and righteousness stands at a distance; for truth stumbles in the public square, and uprightness cannot enter. Truth is lacking, and whoever turns from evil is despoiled. The LORD saw it, and it displeased him that there was no justice.—Isaiah 59:4, 9, 14–15 (NRSV)

[Jesus] said to them, "You are the ones who justify yourselves in the eyes of men, but God knows your hearts. What is highly valued among men is detestable in God's sight.—Luke 16:15

They made her stand before the group and said to Jesus, "Teacher, this woman was caught in the act of adultery. In the Law Moses commanded us to stone such women. Now what do you say?" They were using this question as a trap, in order to have a basis for accusing him. But Jesus bent down and started to write on the ground with his finger. When they kept on questioning him, he straightened up and said to them, "If any one of you is without sin, let him be the first to throw a stone at her." Again he stooped down and wrote on the ground. At this, those who heard began to go away one at a time, the older ones first, until only Jesus was left, with the woman still standing there. Jesus straightened up and asked her, "Woman, where are they? Has no one condemned you?" "No one, sir," she said. "Then, neither do I condemn you," Jesus declared. "Go now and leave your life of sin."—John 8:3–11

But even if you should suffer for what is right, you are blessed. "Do not fear what they fear; do not be frightened."—1 Peter 3:14

Practical Counsel

In perhaps no other part of our legal system has the distinction between what is "right" and what is "legal" become more blurred than in the arena of criminal law. The meaning of the treasured American constitutional right of a person charged with a crime to a fair and swift trial before a jury of peers, a trial in which that defendant is "presumed innocent until proven guilty," has become distorted. It's almost as if we've come to believe that the presumption of innocence applies not only to the judicial system, but to our own consciences and hearts as well.

At a certain level, as Christians, we all understand guilt. We understand that each of us has sinned against God, that none of us but Jesus Christ could live a sinless life. And we understand that God, in his infinite mercy, sent the innocent Jesus to die for us on the cross, to receive the punishment we deserved, to stand in our place in the ultimate act of love. But to accept this gift of grace, to even begin to comprehend it, we must first acknowledge our own guilt before God. Confessing our own guilt is an essential step to salvation. Without conviction, from what are we set free? A person who stubbornly denies his or her own guilt before a holy God is really denying Christ, saying to Christ, in effect, "You died in vain, I don't need you."

Under God's justice system, if I deny my own guilt, I disqualify myself from God's saving grace. Instead, as Christians, in the moment of salvation, we throw ourselves on the mercy of the court. We plead "guilty as charged." It is only from that point God's redemptive mercy seals our fate. It is only from that point we can even begin to truly grasp that the shed blood of Jesus Christ is the *only* thing sparing us from the eternal punishment we deserve.

So what about in the secular legal system? If, as a Christian believer, I am charged with a crime, what do I do? Am I automatically "innocent until proven guilty"? Do I fight the charges tooth and nail every step of the way, because that is my "right" as an American? Or do I search my heart? Do I ask myself the hard questions: "Did I commit a crime?" "Do I have the courage to take responsibility for my actions?" "Will my reaction to these charges glorify Jesus Christ?"

I want to be very clear on this. I am not advocating that Christians take the fall for crimes they did not commit. When the apostle Paul was facing a multitude of criminal charges, he claimed the full rights of his Roman citizenship, for procedural advantage. But Paul was seeking merely to protect himself from arbitrary punishment without trial, and to protect himself from being tried for unspecified and unsubstantiated charges. So he appealed again and again, fully exercising his rights. And at every step of the way, before each tribunal, Paul shared his testimony of faith, explaining carefully and honestly those acts that he did and didn't commit.

The last seven and one half chapters of the book of Acts consist mostly of the record of Paul's trials and appeals. So certainly, no Christian should be expected to simply accept punishment for someone else's crimes, or to suffer the deprivation of the constitutional rights afforded to American citizens.

But, by contrast, it is important to note that Paul never shirked responsibility for the things he *did* do. He openly admitted his service to the cause of Jesus Christ, to teaching and spreading the message of the cross. And although the system treated Paul harshly, Paul responded with respect and kindness to even his jailers and guards. Not only was Paul honest, but he understood that his conduct would be a living testimony for Christ. Everyone knew that Paul could talk the talk, but the way he handled himself in the face of criminal charges demonstrated to a skeptical world that he could also walk the walk. Even in the most challenging circumstances, Paul placed his personal integrity, his witness for Christ, above his own freedom.

Imagine what our criminal justice system would look like if people who committed crimes would routinely turn themselves in! Or even if they would simply plead guilty when arrested for a crime they had, in fact, committed. Sure, it's an unrealistic vision, but think of the vast amount of economic and emotional resources that could be saved if our court systems weren't clogged with defendants denying responsibility for their own conduct. Think of the victims of crime who would be spared the fear and agony of reliving their own suffering as they testified against guilty perpetrators in open court. Think of the healing that could occur if those who committed crimes would not only acknowledge and confess their own guilt, but would work diligently to restore their victims' losses.

Maybe the vision I've outlined is hopelessly naive. But maybe not, at least not entirely. Imagine what the world would look like if even those of us who profess to be Christians would begin to take full responsibility for our own criminal conduct. How many traffic cops would be spared from wasting their valuable time in court hearings over speeding tickets? How many fraudulent investment or marketing schemes could be put out of operation before the next innocent person gets scammed? How many young people could be saved from the trauma of physical abuse at the hands of a trusted church member or leader? Sadly, Christians are not above committing crimes, regardless of how highly we might regard ourselves. The real question is, can we deal with our transgressions in a way that would honor Christ, or do we simply jump on the world's bandwagon, hire the best criminal defense lawyers we can afford, and loudly proclaim our innocence, no matter who else gets hurt?

Now, again, it is important for me to clarify something. I am not condemning those attorneys who practice criminal defense law. There is certainly ample biblical justification for Christians to take on the holy calling of defending the innocent, the oppressed, and the weak. Even Jesus himself stepped in to defend the woman who had been charged with adultery. But I would note that Jesus did not encourage her to falsely proclaim her innocence. Rather, he expertly and effectively appealed to the sensibilities of those who were about to render punishment for her crime. Jesus is a champion of justice, and justice is where we need to keep our focus. Sometimes justice demands a vigorous defense, sometimes justice demands a fair and skillfully negotiated plea agreement, and sometimes justice demands an unconditional confession.

If I were charged with a crime (whether the charges were true or false), the first person I would contact would be a trusted and capable criminal defense attorney who shared my Christian beliefs. Since I do not practice criminal law, legal counsel would be essential for me to fully understand the potential consequences of the charges, how the criminal justice process would likely unfold, and what the possibilities might be for confession and restoration. Plus, an experienced criminal defense attorney would be able to help prevent me from being improperly treated on my journey through the law enforcement, court, and prison systems. But once I came to an understanding of the situation, I hope and pray that God would grant me the courage to face the matter with Christ-honoring integrity. And I hope and pray that anyone facing such circumstances as they read these words will earnestly pray for that courage as well.

CHAPTER 5

The Estate-Planning Illusion

> Do not store up for yourselves treasures on earth, where moth
> and rust destroy, and where thieves break in and steal. But store
> up for yourselves treasures in heaven, where moth and rust
> do not destroy, and where thieves do not break in and steal.
> For where your treasure is, there your heart will be also.
>
> —MATTHEW 6:19–21

Life Lessons—Ed and Elsa

"I'm sorry, Mike, we'd really like to help in a bigger way, but we're just not able to," Ed apologized as he put down the phone. And they weren't empty words. He and Elsa had been thrilled when they heard that Mike, a young man they used to teach in junior high Sunday school class, had become a full-time missionary to the rural poor in Central Appalachia. And now that Mike was raising funds for the renovation of the flood-damaged Christian medical clinic where he served as pharmacist, chaplain, and live-in custodian, they really did wish they could give more than a token donation. But it just wasn't possible. *How ironic,* Ed thought to himself, as he gazed around his comfortable home, *all we've been blessed with, and yet so little left to give.*

Just then, the phone rang again. "Hi, Dad!" crackled the voice of Ed and Elsa's son, Evan, a successful doctor living in a nearby city. "I just wanted to let you know we've all arrived safely in the Bahamas. The sun is shining, our hotel is top notch, and the kids are already in the pool. After the super buffet dinner, Ellen and I are going downstairs to try our luck in the casino for the evening, so I wanted to catch you and Mom now. Talk to you next week when we get back. Bye!" Ed had hardly had a chance to say a word. And now he began to ponder.

He and Elsa loved their three children. They were good kids, all completing college and graduate degrees with flying colors, and all keeping in touch regularly, getting together on holidays and special occasions. And the grandkids were wonderful, all showing every sign of following in their parents' footsteps. Sure, there were some things that bothered Ed and Elsa about the children—they wished they would get more involved in their churches, and perhaps live a little more modestly (there always seemed to be an expensive new car in their garages or another fancy vacation in the works)—but wasn't that why Ed and Elsa had worked so hard all their lives, so the kids would have it a little easier? *Wasn't it?* Ed thought to himself, images flashing in his mind over and over again of Mike working so hard to share the gospel down in that miserable flooded-out Appalachian medical clinic.

But, Ed reminded himself, *there's nothing I can do now. I'm retired. What's done is done.* The advisers from the estate-planning firm his son-in-law recommended had taken care of that. Now everything was signed, sealed, and delivered. The plan was in place.

At first, all the estate-planning talk had seemed to make so much sense to Ed and Elsa. At the initial meeting with them, the advisers started by describing in graphic detail what might happen to Ed and Elsa's estate if they failed to plan. Full-color pie charts were on display, showing huge chunks of wealth ending up in the hands of Uncle Sam and probate lawyers. Other risks, like medical expenses and lawsuits, were presented in frightening detail, with newspaper and magazine articles documenting the reality of the danger.

At their next meeting, over a nice lunch at a local restaurant, the advisers steered the conversation into a long discussion about how unfair and unjust "the system" is, and how so many families get soaked, while certain others manage to shrewdly protect what they own. Soon, the advisers had Ed and Elsa feeling very vulnerable, like they had to do something quickly to protect everything they had worked so hard to accumulate. Near the end of the lunch meeting, one of the advisers even quoted the Bible, talking about how God wants us to be as wise as serpents, and how principles of good stewardship demanded aggressive action. And Ed and Elsa were hooked.

So, over the next several weeks, Ed and Elsa eagerly awaited the unveiling of a comprehensive estate plan to protect their wealth and thereby provide security for their family. And they weren't disappointed. The advisers had a whole series of recommendations: the purchase of extensive life insurance and the creation of an irrevocable life insurance trust to provide tax-free liquidity to the family upon the deaths of Ed and Elsa; the purchase of long-term annuities to provide a fixed-income stream for Ed and Elsa while insulating the principal from risk; the placing of many other assets into a series of trusts for the benefit of each grandchild, to minimize taxation; the transfer of the title of the family home into a family partnership composed of all three children and their spouses, to avoid probate and reduce valuation; and the transfer of virtually all remaining assets into a family legacy trust to be co-managed by Ed and Elsa and the estate-planning firm, to provide for continuity of management as Ed and Elsa aged and to make sure the family wealth was secure for all the future generations.

The plan would be expensive to implement. There were significant legal fees to be paid for drafting the necessary documents. There were large premiums for the life insurance and commissions for the investments. And the estate-planning firm would not only need to be paid for its services in creating and implementing the plan, but also for its ongoing services in managing the trusts. But Ed and Elsa bit the bullet and spent the money, feeling it was the only reasonable way to attain the protection they so badly wanted. And the plan was implemented. Everything was restructured. The cost was high, but security had been attained, it seemed.

But now, with the echoes of his telephone conversations with the disappointed young missionary and his own luxury-loving son still ringing in his ears, Ed began to question. *How far would the small fortune Elsa and I spent on our estate plan have gone in refurbishing the mission clinic? Will more wealth really benefit our children and grandchildren, or is it actually going to poison them? Do Elsa and I really want to spend the rest of our lives living on a modest fixed income, without the control and freedom we once had to use our wealth to benefit God's kingdom where and when God led us? Was our estate planning guided by abiding trust in God's provision, or by greed and panic? Did we really stop to think and pray about what we were doing? Did we substitute the illusion of worldly security for genuine faith in God?* Ed sat quietly for another moment, then whispered to himself, "Oh, well, what's done is done."

More Life Lessons—James and Jeannette

"Thanks for seeing us so soon! We have a lot of questions—things we need to get in the works right away to protect our estate!" exclaimed James, as attorney Rochelle Roberts entered the brightly lit contemporary conference room of her firm's suburban office suite.

James and Jeannette Jenkins had known Rochelle informally for several years through some mutual church activities, but they had never met with her in a professional legal capacity. Before Rochelle even had a chance to take her seat at the sleek glass table and open the thin folder she was carrying, James began waving around an article he had clipped from a magazine for retired military veterans, telling Rochelle urgently, "This is what we want. We need to set up a plan like this to protect ourselves and our kids!"

Rochelle smiled warmly toward James and Jeannette as she gently accepted the article James was thrusting toward her, gracefully slipping it into the folder on the table. "Well, aren't you going to read it?" James quickly asked, looking somewhat insulted.

"Oh, I'll read it, James. I'll be sure to read it," Rochelle responded confidently, "but it's not time for that yet. We have some things to talk about first."

James protested immediately. "Rochelle, I thought you were an attorney we could work with, someone who could help us. But now you're telling me you won't do what we came here to do? I said I want a plan just like the one in the article. Isn't that clear enough for you?"

"James," Rochelle began again, very calmly, "let me make you a promise. If you bear with me while I ask you and Jeannette to consider some very important questions, then I'll read your article and if that's still the plan you want by the time we're finished, I'll help you set it up. But first we need to talk. When you called me to ask whether I handle estate-planning matters I said 'yes,' and that's what I hope to do. But I cannot help you plan your estate in a competent manner without first understanding the context, your own unique combination of circumstances, the values, goals, and needs you and Jeannette share."

"All right, have it your way—you're the lawyer," James finally conceded. So Rochelle seized the opening and began a long and wide-ranging discussion with James and Jeannette, asking them questions about their financial status, their health, their hopes and goals for retirement, their children and grandchildren, their involvement with and support for charitable organizations, and their fears and concerns about aging. As the discussion continued, Jeannette, who had been very timid and quiet at first, gradually relaxed and began to share right along with James, who was never at a loss for words.

During the hour-long discussion, Rochelle discovered that James was in surprisingly frail health, with some serious heart problems, but that Jeannette was almost eight years younger than her husband and in excellent health. She learned that Jeannette had grown up in very difficult economic circumstances and now, having achieved a modestly comfortable lifestyle, was very risk-averse and enjoyed being fully in control of her financial affairs. She found out that the four Jenkins children were grown and independent, all well established with families of their own. And she found that James and Jeannette had a special love for a national Christian ministry serving military officers and their families, and had often supported that ministry prayerfully and financially over the years.

As the end of the hour finally approached, Rochelle said, "Okay, before we forget, let me take a look at this article." Her experienced eyes quickly scanned the text, and she instantly recognized the familiar approach being used by the author of the article, a financial planner promoting the use of an estate plan involving some special products his firm had developed (and upon the sale of which, coincidentally, his firm would earn a handsome commission). The article employed a number of common scare tactics, focusing especially on the potentially horrific impact of federal estate taxes, and then presented the plan in question as if it were the only viable alternative. Rochelle smiled to herself.

"James," she began diplomatically, "do you realize that the federal tax the author is writing about in this article applies only to very large estates, estates at least five times larger than yours? And that it would cost many thousands of dollars in fees and commissions to set up a plan like that, plus annual costs for the ongoing administration? And that under that plan, half of everything you and Jeannette own would be tied up in a restricted trust after you die? And that the author didn't even seem to consider the possibility of charitable gifting in designing his plan? And . . ."

Rochelle stopped her speech abruptly as James suddenly reached across the table and snatched the article from her hands, crumpling it up into a ball, a big grin spreading across his face. "Rochelle, I guess I owe you an apology," he said sheepishly, as Jeannette nodded knowingly.

"No problem, James, just doing my job," Rochelle replied graciously. "Now let's make an appointment for next week, so we can get started with a simple estate plan I'm envisioning that will meet *your* needs, and save you a lot of money and frustration."

Biblical Insights

Go to the ant, you sluggard; consider its ways and be wise! It has no commander, no overseer or ruler, yet it stores its provisions in summer and gathers its food at harvest.—Proverbs 6:6–8

A good man leaves an inheritance for his children's children.—Proverbs 13:22

Do not wear yourself out to get rich; have the wisdom to show restraint. Cast but a glance at riches, and they are gone, for they will surely sprout wings and fly off to the sky like an eagle.—Proverbs 23:4–5

No one can serve two masters. Either he will hate the one and love the other, or he will be devoted to the one and despise the other. You cannot serve both God and Money.—Matthew 6:24

Then he said to them, "Watch out! Be on your guard against all kinds of greed; a man's life does not consist in the abundance of his possessions.—Luke 12:15

Brothers and sisters, I give an example from daily life: once a person's will has been ratified, no one adds to it or annuls it.—Galatians 3:15 (NRSV)

See to it that no one takes you captive through hollow and deceptive philosophy, which depends on human tradition and the basic principles of this world rather than on Christ.—Colossians 2:8

Command those who are rich in this present world not to be arrogant nor to put their hope in wealth, which is so uncertain, but to put their hope in God, who richly provides us with everything for our enjoyment.—1 Timothy 6:17

Practical Counsel

The concept of estate planning is sound and biblical. In the Old Testament and the New, we are encouraged to plan wisely for the future, to soberly count the costs before we proceed. God's Word even suggests we should seek to leave an inheritance for the generations who will follow us. So it certainly makes sense for us, as Christians, to set up careful plans for the distribution of our material wealth upon our inevitable departure from this world. If nothing else, an estate plan represents a final act of good stewardship of those things God has entrusted into our care during this life.

At its core, estate planning is the implementation of a legally binding plan for the disposition of our possessions and property upon death. And most estate plans that are properly arranged address lifetime illness or incapacity as well. Therefore, the typical estate plan might include such elements as a will, a trust, a durable general power of attorney, and an advance directive for health care decision making. The planning process would also generally involve an evaluation of the form of ownership of existing assets, the possibility of making strategic transfers and gifting, and the review of other relevant considerations, such as life insurance, qualified retirement plans, and the appointment of fiduciaries (executors, trustees, and guardians for minor children) as necessary. Again, estate planning of this nature is entirely consistent with a responsible Christian worldview.

Where Christians need to be careful when it comes to estate planning is in the perspective, or heart attitude, with which we carry out the planning process. Far too many Christians end up falling for the same psychological ploys as the rest of society, creating estate plans based on an unholy combination of fear and greed rather than on principles of wise and constructive planning. And far too many Christians are drawn deeper and deeper into this spirit of fear and greed by an estate-planning industry built largely on selling the illusions of "protection" and "security" to the very people it has just worked quite diligently to frighten.

The sales technique commonly used by many in the estate-planning industry (including both attorney and non-attorney estate planners) is to create an artificial sense of panic or vulnerability in clients, based on some exaggerated threat to their material wealth, or that of their eventual heirs. The bogeyman could be taxes, or liability risk from potential lawsuits, or probate costs, or nursing care expenses, or changing economic conditions—the list goes on and on, limited only by the creativity of the salesperson.

Once the threat has been sufficiently established in the client's mind, the planner moves to the greed phase of the sales pitch. The slightest possibility of the loss of any portion of the client's estate to the threat in question is painted as grossly unfair, confiscatory, even morally wrong. And the client is encouraged to think that exposing the estate even slightly to the risk in question would be utterly foolish, a sign of weakness or irresponsibility, or even bad stewardship. And now, with the near-panicked emotions of the client having been carefully cultivated to the point they most closely resemble those of a toddler tightly clutching a disputed toy and shouting, "Mine!" the salesperson moves into the last phase of the sales pitch.

Finally, the increasingly desperate client is offered relief. The relief can come in as many different forms as the threat. It might be a complex trust arrangement, or a big second-to-die life insurance policy, or an annuity, or an offshore asset transfer. But regardless of the form the relief takes, it will always appear to provide the client with protection. And at this point, the client is willing to pay dearly for security. In fact, the client is willing to pay not only the direct monetary cost required but is also willing to take on the burden of added accounting complexity, or reduced liquidity, or exposure to new risks (risks which, almost invariably, are already being developed into a truly terrifying new bogeyman by some other estate planner getting ready for the next big sales pitch), or any number of other tangible and intangible costs of the estate-planning technique being implemented.

The specific estate-planning tools are not what I am calling into question. It's the perspective. While the words *protection* and *security* might sound innocent enough, as Christians we know they represent false promises. When we put our trust in them, they become idols. The only real protection and security we have are in the promises of Jesus Christ. Everything else will wither away or burn up, or be consumed by moths or rust. So, when the promises being sold by the estate-planning industry are protection and security, we need to be fully aware that a deception is at hand, and act accordingly.

With our faith and trust in Christ, we can and should make reasonable attempts to plan for our families, loved ones, and favorite charities, in accordance with our consciences and circumstances.

But our goal should be stewardship and provision in reliance on God's providence, not protection and security in reliance on the feeble promises of men, governments, and other institutions. Our real treasures need to be in heaven, not here on earth.

When we do our estate planning with the constant awareness of God's sovereignty, we can approach the entire process with joy and freedom. We won't be susceptible to the fear- and greed-driven fads and gimmicks that periodically cycle through the estate-planning industry and are so earnestly promoted to us, sometimes right inside our own churches. We can focus instead on the needs we hope to meet, the people we hope to bless (this could mean leaving them less, not more), and the impact our estate might have in glorifying Christ.

Estate planning is a complex area of the law and every person's situation will present unique opportunities and challenges. We need to plan sensibly, and then entrust our financial future to God. We can experience the peace and serenity God wants for us when we remember that our lives do not consist of our possessions but of our relationship to him.

CHAPTER 6

The Living-Trust Hard Sell

Provide purses for yourselves that will not wear out, a treasure in Heaven
that will not be exhausted, where no thief comes near and no moth
destroys. For where your treasure is, there your heart will be also.

—LUKE 12:33–34

Life Lessons—Walt and Wanda

It wasn't even noon yet, but the banquet room at the Towne Tavern was packed. As they worked their way between crowded tables, looking for a place to sit, Walt and Wanda Webber nodded cheerfully to friends and casual acquaintances. *Wow, everyone we know seems to be here!* Walt thought to himself as Wanda tugged on his arm. She had just spotted their next-door neighbors from the condo, Bill and Betty Benson, at a table along the far wall, and Bill was gesturing, holding up two fingers, inviting the Webbers to join them.

As Walt and Wanda thankfully settled in at the Bensons' table, the couples began to talk. Both had seen the ad in the local newspaper for the free lunch and asset-protection planning seminar. They all laughed as they joked about being retired and never turning down a chance at free food, especially food from the Towne Tavern, one of the best restaurants in the area. And, seeing so many other local retired folks present, everyone felt reassured they had made the right choice.

The table conversation was light and the food delicious as lunchtime quickly passed. Soon the sponsors of the event formally introduced themselves and thanked everyone for coming. There were three men, all "asset-protection planning experts" from an insurance company based in a nearby state, and a woman who identified herself as an attorney with offices in a nearby city. As each spoke, the others circulated the room, busily handing out brochures and small wrapped gifts with printed tags to each couple or individual in attendance.

Soon the lights dimmed and an engaging video began, with narration by a famous actor. The video was called "Ten Things the Government and Your Lawyer Don't Want You to Know." As the video finished, the three "experts" launched into a fast-moving, high-tech, tag-team presentation, with colorful slides, charts, and graphs sprinkled throughout, along with images of troubling news headlines about probate, wills, taxes, lawsuits, and lawyers. The attorney didn't speak, but frequently nodded her head in grave affirmation as the presentation unfolded.

The message was clear to everyone in the room: You are at risk, your assets are at risk, your lifestyle is at risk, and you need to do something about it. If you don't do something, you are cheating yourselves, your children, and your grandchildren out of all you and they deserve. And you can't rely on the people you've trusted in the past to advise you on matters of estate planning, because they are part of the problem—your lawyer, your accountant, your financial adviser—they're all just lining up for their piece of the action. You have to do something before it's too late, and we can help you.

By midafternoon Walt, like most of the other guests, was feeling very unsettled, full of questions and concerns. *Why didn't anybody warn me about this before? And what about my lawyer, Jake Jordan—I've known him for twenty years, I see him most Sundays at church and most Thursdays at our Rotary Club meetings, but Jake never told me about any of this!* Meanwhile, Wanda was listening intently, hanging on every word from the speakers' lips, waiting for them to reveal the solution, the remedy, the way for her and Walt to protect themselves and their heirs against all this unacceptable risk.

Finally, the entire afternoon reached a crescendo as the grand and elegant tool, the one thing with the power sufficient to resolve all the problems and eliminate virtually all the risks, was, at long last, unveiled. It was called the "living trust." And now the presentation moved to an even higher level of energy and intensity. The sense of urgency, the excitement, and the passion of the experts for this living trust was uncontainable—they smiled and laughed and congratulated each other as they quickly explained how the living trust would slay the dragon of taxes, bypass the horrors of probate, and, best of all, keep the lawyers permanently at bay. Tens or even hundreds of thousands of dollars would be saved! Maybe even millions! By this time, almost everyone in the room was enthusiastically nodding their heads along with the speakers, including Walt and Wanda. There was audible laughter and scattered applause breaking out.

But now there was some bad news. "Because of unavoidable scheduling difficulties," the attorney announced soberly, "I have to take our three experts to the regional airport later tonight, and it might be months before their schedules will permit them to return to our area." Normally, she explained, the experts would have made themselves available on the day after the presentation to meet with interested individuals, answer their questions, and, if desired, assist them in setting up living trusts. But, she continued apologetically, "Now they can only be with us for the few remaining hours this afternoon."

One of the experts then chimed in, echoing the attorney's apologetic tone, "All of us were very disappointed about this situation, so we wanted to do something special to make it up to each of you, to thank you for the time you've invested with us today. If you would now pick up the little gift we gave you earlier, the one with the tag that says 'Please Do Not Open Until Instructed.' Here is what we are able to do, in appreciation for any inconvenience we may have caused—inside each gift you will find a certificate, a very valuable certificate, redeemable today, for a discount of anywhere from 10 percent to 50 percent off our regular fees for a living trust."

The room quickly filled with the sound of tearing paper. Walt and Wanda smiled as Bill and Betty Benson waved their 10 percent certificate, then Wanda excitedly withdrew a 50 percent certificate from her box, exclaiming, "Hey, look, it's our lucky day!"

As the room returned to order, the speakers promptly concluded the program, leaving as much time as possible, they said, to meet with those interested in establishing a living trust, on a first-come, first-served basis. A passing reference was made to the standard fee schedule included in the materials passed out earlier in the afternoon, and a waiting line quickly formed. The three experts each sat facing wide tables, surrounded with stacks of shiny three-ring binders and glossy paper, sleek computers, and high-speed printers. Each expert talked with interested couples or individuals, one after another, while the attorney roved among them all, witnessing signatures on fresh documents and answering questions.

As Walt and Wanda stood in line, they chatted quietly about the price. "Even with the discount, it's still a couple of thousand bucks—are you sure you want to go ahead?" Walt asked.

"Oh, Walt, just relax," Wanda replied. "Look at the thousands and thousands we'll save our kids—I know a good deal when I see it, and this is a good deal. And if we don't take it, someone behind us will—and look at the time, it's almost 6:30—I hope they can get us in before it's too late."

About forty-five minutes later, Walt and Wanda walked back to their car in the restaurant parking lot, clutching a black notebook with gold lettering, full of papers they had signed but never read. On the way home, they stopped at another favorite restaurant for a late dinner, to celebrate their accomplishments of the day. When they finally returned to the condo, they carefully placed the notebook on a shelf near their writing desk, intending to peruse it some rainy day.

And it was on that very shelf, some six years later, that Walt and Wanda's son, Wayne, found the notebook, undisturbed. *Well,* Wayne thought, *I'd better bring this to the lawyer's office, with the rest of the papers—it looks like it could be important. I recall Mom and Dad bragging to me about how they were going to save all these taxes and probate costs and lawyers' fees with this living trust they had set up.*

Later that day, Wayne sat in a law firm conference room with Jake Jordan, the attorney he'd always remembered as handling his parents' legal affairs. After some condolences about Walt's recent death and a few minutes of reminiscing, they agreed Walt was surely glad to be together again with Wanda, who had died just the year before. "And," added Jake reassuringly, "I was with your Dad at that men's retreat where we both gave our lives to Christ, twenty-some years ago, so I feel quite certain of where he is now."

Wayne and Jake spent the next few hours delving into all his late parents' papers, identifying assets, liabilities, and relevant documents. As they had nearly completed that process, Jake explained to Wayne, "I can surmise now precisely what happened with this living trust. Since I was never informed about it and I don't recognize the names of any of the witnesses, I suspect that your parents got lured into one of those fly-by-night estate-planning seminars—the ones where they give you a 'free' lunch and then scare you with all kinds of exaggerated horror stories about probate and taxes and lawyers. Then they use a slick sales pitch to get you to drop thousands of dollars on a generic living trust. And then they leave town as quick as they came in.

"But it's what they don't tell you that's the killer—they don't tell you that for people like your parents, the living trust saves no taxes at all, and they don't tell you that you have to re-title all your assets into the name of the living trust for it to be effective, and they don't tell you that you'll probably still need a lawyer and a will to settle your estate anyway, even if your living trust is valid. But in this case, the whole matter is very clear-cut. Since your parents never bothered to legally transfer any of their assets into the living trust, it's totally worthless. Whatever money they spent on it may as well have been thrown down the sewer. I've seen this kind of thing before. It's too bad. But as long as there are unscrupulous 'estate planners' or 'asset-protection experts' or whatever the living trust salesmen have decided to call themselves these days, I'm sure I'll see it again."

More Life Lessons—Bill and Betty

Bill and Betty Benson sat through the very same "estate-planning" presentation as Walt and Wanda Webber. And they experienced almost all the same reactions and emotions as Walt and Wanda and everyone else in the room at the Towne Tavern. They were fearful and outraged about the risk to their assets apparently posed by taxes and lawyers and the probate process. And they wanted to do something about it, and quickly. Bill and Betty had both suffered from some serious health problems since retirement, and they knew they didn't have forever to act. And this living trust sounded like the perfect solution.

But, when Betty opened her checkbook at the conclusion of the seminar and glanced at the ledger, she saw that the account balance was short by about $1,000 from the price on the standard fee schedule for a living trust, even after applying the 10 percent discount she and Bill had qualified for. And as she and Bill remained seated, discussing their options, the "first-come, first-served" line began to grow. The Bensons had a credit card, but tried to use it only for emergencies and, even then, only when they had cash available to pay off the bill as soon as it arrived. They had some money in CDs, but there would be an early withdrawal penalty if they accessed those funds. Their other investments were even less liquid. And Bill's next pension check wasn't due for another few weeks. More time passed and by now the line had grown very long.

Finally, Bill made a decision. "Betty, we know at least three different lawyers right here in this town. There's that young guy at church—he seems pretty sharp—and there's that woman in your aerobics class—you're always saying something nice about her—and then there's that couple we met volunteering at the Salvation Army—isn't the husband a law professor? Anyhow, tomorrow I'm gonna pick up the phone and make a few calls. If this living-trust thing is all it's cracked up to be, I'm sure one of them can point us in the right direction. For now, let's go home and get some supper!"

The next morning, Bill did pick up the phone. He found the number of the young lawyer from church. Although it turned out the young lawyer didn't practice estate-planning law, he put Bill through to one of his partners who did. That partner assured Bill he had done the right thing by not purchasing the living trust the night before, explaining that time-pressured selling techniques were typical of unscrupulous living-trust promoters, and that the story about the airport and the special one-day discounts sounded very suspicious. He also said he could make some discreet inquiries about the reputation of the attorney who participated in the seminar and get back to Bill. Bill thanked him for his help and asked him to proceed.

Next, Bill called the attorney from Betty's aerobics class. When he eventually got through, she seemed unusually interested in hearing the details of the previous afternoon. But then she advised Bill she didn't practice estate-planning law and didn't know much about living trusts herself. Bill asked, somewhat confused, "Why are you so interested in the details of what happened at that seminar, if you don't even work in this field of law?"

She answered, "Mr. Benson, I hope you don't feel I've wasted your time, but you see, I'm the president of our county bar association. We're just in the midst of forming a task force to better educate the public about living trusts and their uses and misuses. It seems so many of our member attorneys have had clients victimized by living-trust promoters.

"We're also communicating with the consumer protection division of the state attorney general's office, and we've learned they're investigating several out-of-state companies that operate on and off right here in our county. There may very well end up being criminal charges filed, under our unfair and deceptive trade practices laws, because of the misleading sales techniques being employed, and because of the false and exaggerated claims being made about the effectiveness of the living trust in avoiding or reducing taxes and other expenses. I was fascinated with your story, Mr. Benson, because it sounded like something ripped right from the pages of our task force case files."

"So, you think we did the right thing by not purchasing the living trust?" Bill asked.

"Well," the attorney responded, "as I said, I don't practice estate-planning law and I don't know whether you should have a living trust, but I can tell you that many people in our county have been taken advantage of by the living-trust industry, and I'm glad to hear that you and Betty are not among them."

Bill was feeling better about things now, but he still remembered what the experts at the seminar had said, how they warned that many lawyers would be hostile toward living trusts. Supposedly, the experts asserted, the living trusts were cutting into the attorneys' pocketbooks and wallets, because once the living trusts were in place, further legal services would not be required, especially at death. *Could this be why the practicing attorneys I've talked with are so negative about living trusts?* he thought. *Is it just biased self-interest?*

With this one lingering concern on his mind, Bill tracked down the number of the local university and navigated his way through the directory to the office phone of the law professor they met at the Salvation Army. Like the bar association president, the professor seemed unusually interested in the details of Bill's story.

After listening intently to Bill, the professor began, "Bill, it's providential that you chose to call me about this issue. You see, I never practiced law privately and I really don't care what makes money for lawyers and what doesn't. In fact, my primary training is in taxation and actuarial matters—I'm really more of a mathematician than an attorney, although I hold two law degrees. But right now I have a student I'm advising with respect to his graduate thesis. Although the study he's undertaken is extremely technical and full of numbers and life-expectancy tables and computer-generated projections, here's what I think might interest you.

"You see, what this student is attempting to quantify is whether an average person would be economically better off with or without a living trust! Because each state has different procedural requirements for probate, his study is based on data collected here in our state. He's being very conservative, assuming a best-case scenario for the money-saving claims made by many living-trust promoters. Then he's factoring in typical up-front costs, including asset transfer expenses of a living trust, compared with a traditional estate plan using wills. Then he's utilizing standard life-expectancy tables and various projected rates of return on investment to calculate the net present value of the purported future savings of probate costs under the living-trust scenario, bearing in mind that the tax consequences of the living trust are neutral because the same tax savings can generally be achieved using traditional estate-planning tools. And, of course, please remember that the analysis of the data so far is preliminary.

"But here's what the study appears to show: Living trusts result in no net economic benefit. In simple terms, instead of spending more dollars today to set up a living trust, with the hope your heirs will come out ahead in the long run, you—and your heirs—will probably be better off spending fewer dollars on a simpler estate plan today and investing the savings. If you want, I could send you some sample calculations and a more detailed mathematical model."

"Wow," Bill replied with a chuckle, "that was more than I ever bargained for, and no, the sample calculations won't be necessary!"

The professor paused for a moment, perhaps slightly puzzled why anyone wouldn't jump at the chance to review his sample calculations, then said matter-of-factly, "Well, I have a class in six minutes, so I have to run. Let me know if you need anything else!"

As soon as Bill put down the phone, it rang. It was the estate-planning lawyer, the one who was checking on the reputation of the attorney who'd been involved in the living-trust seminar. "Here's what I learned," he told Bill. "She's been admitted to practice for three years, and she's already been placed on disciplinary probation once for an ethics violation. Not only that—her advertising materials list her primary area of practice as criminal defense law. I asked around with a couple of my reputable estate-planning contacts in the city and no one seems to know her. Also, she's not a member of our county Estate Planning Council. Quite frankly, Bill, I think she was just lending her name and law license to the living-trust seminar to make a few quick bucks and keep the insurance guys out of hot water for practicing law without a license. That's my best guess."

"All right, thank you," Bill replied. "And I was wondering—could my wife and I make an appointment to come down there and have you review our estate plan sometime?"

"Sure," the lawyer answered, but added mischievously, "but I don't provide a free lunch!"

Biblical Insights

The discerning heart seeks knowledge, but the mouth of a fool feeds on folly.—Proverbs 15:14

Whoever loves money never has money enough; whoever loves wealth is never satisfied with his income. This too is meaningless.—Ecclesiastes 5:10

Wisdom, like an inheritance, is a good thing and benefits those who see the sun. Wisdom is a shelter as money is a shelter, but the advantage of knowledge is this: that wisdom preserves the life of its possessor. —Ecclesiastes 7:11–12

Since you trust in your deeds and riches, you too will be taken captive. —Jeremiah 48:7

And [Jesus] told them this parable: "The ground of a certain rich man produced a good crop. He thought to himself, 'What shall I do? I have no place to store my crops.' Then he said, 'This is what I'll do. I will tear down my barns and build bigger ones, and there I will store all my grain and my goods. And I'll say to myself, 'You have plenty of good things laid up for many years. Take life easy; eat, drink and be merry.' But God said to him, 'You fool! This very night your life will be demanded from you. Then who will get what you have prepared for yourself?' This is how it will be with anyone who stores up things for himself but is not rich toward God.—Luke 12:16–21

Practical Counsel

The reason the living trust merits a separate chapter in this book isn't because of what the living trust is or what it isn't. It's simply because the living trust is so often overused and abused, even within Christian estate-planning circles.

It would also be wise at this point, in order to prevent confusion, to quickly distinguish the living trust from the living will, which is an entirely different animal discussed in chapter 8. A simple way to keep the two concepts distinct would be to think of the living trust as dealing with your assets (real estate, money, investments, and so forth), while the living will deals with your body (medical treatment decisions).

Now, getting back to the living trust, let's envision the estate-planning attorney as a carpenter with a box full of tools. Some of the tools in the box might include traditional wills, durable powers of attorney, advanced health care directives, testamentary trusts, charitable trusts, irrevocable trusts, conveyances, gifting strategies, entity formation, asset re-titling, life insurance, and so on. Nestled among all the other tools in the box is the living trust.

Make no mistake—the living trust is a legitimate estate-planning tool, a very flexible tool with many uses and many potential benefits. In the hands of a skilled and diligent estate planner, a living trust can enhance the continuity, efficiency, and economy of many estate plans. In some cases, a living trust is just the right tool. But in other cases it won't be necessary or appropriate at all. Unfortunately, the estate-planning community is awash with carpenters who think the living trust is the only tool in their box.

The old saying "If the only tool you have is a hammer, everything starts to look like a nail" summarizes the situation best. For years the living trust has been brought out of the box and presented as the best or only sensible solution in all kinds of situations that would better have been resolved through any number of other means. Sometimes the living trust has made the situations worse. And sadly, coercion, deception, fear, greed, misrepresentation, over-statement, and various other high-pressure sales techniques have often been employed to make sure the living trust was the tool selected, and often at an inflated cost, and often with little or no follow-up assistance in proper implementation.

The concept of a trust can sometimes be a difficult one to grasp. A simple way to envision a trust is to imagine you have a possession of some kind—for purposes of this discussion, let's say $1,000 in cash. When you have the cash in your own wallet, you are the owner. But if you hand the cash over to someone else to manage for you, you have now created a trust. You are the "grantor" or "trustor" and the person holding the cash for your benefit is the "trustee." The arrangement you have with the trustee to manage the cash for your benefit is the "trust." If you are alive when you hand the money over to the trustee, you have created a very simple living trust (albeit one that would be very difficult, if not impossible, to prove or enforce!).

Trusts in various forms have been around for centuries and can be very helpful. Under the right circumstances, a living trust can be the perfect solution to many estate-planning problems and pit-falls. But I include this chapter primarily to expose the abuses that have become so common in the overselling of living trusts as a panacea, the "one size fits all" solution for everyone's estate-planning issues, and also as a warning against falling into the danger-ous trap of worldly worry and the materialistic mind-set so often promoted and encouraged by the sales techniques of the living-trust industry.

The hard-sell approach to living trusts is just another reminder there are many people ready, willing, and able to sell other folks false dreams. Many times, the planning industry (whether it's called estate planning, financial planning, retirement planning, asset-protection planning, probate-avoidance planning, tax planning, secession planning, or some other trendy new name) is built around convincing people they need this or that document, this or that business arrangement, this or that life insurance policy, this or that investment, or this or that living trust—something that will supposedly provide them and their family with lasting security.

But, as the Scriptures warn us, all these humanly arranged devices, all the ways we try to store up and protect earthly wealth, really amount to trying to capture the wind. There's simply no such thing as achieving lasting security from material possessions. While it's certainly wise to plan for the future and use good stewardship to diversify our assets and take advantage of wise planning techniques, we are fools if we place our trust and hope in any worldly wealth. Despite all our best efforts, it can still disappear like the wind.

Throughout the Bible, God encourages us to let go of the false sense of security that money and wealth can bring, to let go of a false dream and focus instead on our relationship with him. As King Solomon said, "Fear God, and keep his commandments; for that is the whole duty of everyone" (Ecclesiastes 12:13 NRSV)— and it's the only thing that will last!

I include this chapter on living trusts with some trepidation, because I know many readers will already have created living trusts for themselves and none of us likes to feel foolish or taken advantage of. As I have stated, it may well be that the living trust in your case was the ideal solution, competently applied by a skilled and ethical estate-planning professional. But for some others, this chapter may represent an unpleasant discovery. When I think about all this, I am drawn to the biblical prophet Jeremiah.

Jeremiah said, "Surely, because you trusted in your strongholds and your treasures, you also shall be taken" (Jeremiah 48:7 NRSV). God used Jeremiah to warn people about the danger of trusting in strongholds and treasures. And I imagine Jeremiah wasn't too popular with those folks, either. Nobody likes being told their priorities are out of whack, and Jeremiah had a way of being especially blunt with people. Now, obviously, I'm not a prophet like Jeremiah and, frankly, I sometimes wish I dared to be as bold and direct as he was, but it's just not the way I usually go about things.

I'll also be the first to admit I'm guilty myself of putting my trust in the wrong places from time to time. There are so many strongholds and treasures we can end up trusting instead of God, besides the obvious things like money and investments, or living trusts, or other humanly devised schemes. All I am proposing is that the living trust be kept in its proper context, that its limitations be candidly acknowledged, and that all of us would endeavor to resist the temptation, whether motivated by fear, or greed, or any other cause, to put unrealistic trust and faith in a frail human contrivance.

Finally, a word of practical counsel to anyone who may already have created a living trust or who might find himself or herself acting as a trustee after the death of the original grantor of a living trust. I strongly advise that you engage qualified, competent legal counsel, as the road ahead of you may have some unexpected twists and turns.

Even in the case where all assets have been properly transferred into the living trust, upon death of the grantor the trustee will be required to handle numerous final details in a process that is nearly identical in many states to that followed by the executor of a traditional probate estate. For example, the trustee will typically need to prepare and file tax returns (quite possibly including death tax returns), the assets of the trust will need to be identified, valued, and safeguarded, and a properly documented plan for distributing what's left of those assets to the heirs (after paying all the expenses) will need to be implemented (either with appropriate court approval or by means of proper agreement of all affected parties).

Being put in charge of handling any estate, whether under a traditional probate scenario or under a living trust, can be a real minefield. If not all the proper steps are followed, the trustee can end up facing personal liability for such things as unpaid debts, unpaid taxes, or improper distributions of assets.

The bottom line is that there is still a great deal of complex work to do when a person who had a living trust dies. Unfortunately, because of the deceptive way living trusts have often been promoted, many folks will be very unpleasantly surprised when the quick, seamless transition they anticipated turns into a much more complicated and extended process.

CHAPTER 7

⚜

The Medicaid-Planning Shell Game

If anyone does not provide for his relatives, and especially for his immediate family, he has denied the faith and is worse than an unbeliever.

—1 TIMOTHY 5:8

Life Lessons—Dan and Dad

"I hate this traffic!" Dan shouted in exasperation, pounding his hand on the steering wheel of his new luxury car.

His monologue of outrage continued in his thoughts as he drove on. *I'm spending more time driving back and forth from this darn nursing home than I actually get to spend there visiting with Dad, and everything else seems to be falling apart . . . Everyone is stressed out at home, things are dropping through the cracks; I don't even know what the kids are doing in the evenings . . . and that new place we built up at the lake is just gathering cobwebs, because I'm getting so far behind with work and stuff I need to get done at home . . .*

It seems like I'm spending half my days on the phone with nursing home administrators and intake social workers, trying to get Dad into a facility closer to us, but all I ever hear about are waiting lists and excuses . . . Boy, when we did all that nursing home planning with Dad and my attorney a few years back, I never expected things to turn out like this . . .

I had no idea nursing homes might not want to take new Medicaid patients when they had plenty of other private-pay patients lining up for their rooms . . . So, sure, now that he needs skilled nursing care, Dad is getting the Medicaid coverage just like we planned for, and, hey, I was able to buy this car and build the cottage on the lake with the money Dad gifted to us as part of the Medicaid qualification strategy, but who ever dreamed I'd spend a year commuting two hours every day through heavy traffic to see Dad? . . . And who ever dreamed Dad would be so unhappy? . . . God, he hates that place, he hates the food, the staff, the doctors . . . the air is stuffy, there's nothing but a brick wall to look at outside his window, and his roommate groans and cries all through the night . . .

Man, I wish we could afford somehow to put him in a private room, but I'd have to sell the place on the lake to do that, and we've barely even used it yet. And now Dad is starting to blame me, asking me why I did this to him, why I made him go to see that 'shyster' lawyer of mine . . . I don't know how much longer I can keep going down there and listening to his complaints and all the guilt he's trying to lay on me . . .

Yes, tonight's gonna have to be the night I break the news to him . . . I just can't keep coming down to see him every day, even though I promised Mom I would . . . I know she would understand if she were still here. Two or maybe three times a week would be enough . . . that's a lot more visits than some of those people in there get. Okay, great, I'm finally here—now to find a parking spot—someplace where I won't get mugged and my car won't get broken into again . . . I hate this neighborhood, I really do . . . I don't know who would ever choose to come here . . .

More Life Lessons—Meg and Mom

Meg's eyes were filling with tears as she walked slowly out from the comfortable reception lobby into the clear spring sunshine. She had intended to get into her car and drive home, but the sight of a peaceful wooden bench surrounded by daffodils in a quiet little spot near the edge of a pond, just beyond the freshly paved and painted parking lot, drew her attention. It had been an overwhelming morning, and her heart was heavy and light all at once. And, more so than anything else, she was suddenly burning with a desire to pray, a desire to enter into a time of deep intimacy with God.

She stepped quietly down a neatly raked woodchip walking path, the fresh scent of newly mown grass lifting lightly on the breeze from the soft green lawns through which the path gently meandered. Reaching the bench, she paused to read the brass lettering on a small plaque: "Donated in Christ's name, with appreciation for all your love and care for our dad—Anonymous." As she sat, the tears that had been welling in her eyes now released in a torrent, and she just let them flow as she closed her eyes and began to pray.

"Dear God, dear Jesus, I just don't know how to thank you enough . . . for your love, for your provision, for your care for me and my mom through this difficult time . . . God, I thank you for the compassion and kindness already being shown Mom on this very first day here at this Christian nursing care center . . . Lord, I know Mom will probably spend her very last months and weeks and days here . . . we don't know how long she has, but you do, and that's okay with me and with her . . . we're at peace and Mom is so looking forward to that moment when she finally meets you face-to-face . . .

"Lord, I want to thank you for all the help, for sending all the people to us who made it possible for Mom to find a spot at this center . . . God, it's so perfect, it's more than we deserve . . . just five minutes from my house, the best staff in the area, the best doctors, Lord, even the food is the best . . . and the Christlike attitude of everyone we meet . . .

"God, I know you provide for even the sparrow in the field, but I want to especially thank you for taking care of the costs of all this for Mom . . . I know it sounds trivial, but I thank you for guiding my dad to buy that long-term care policy for Mom and him before he got sick and passed away three years ago . . . It meant so much to him to know Mom would have the very best care if she ever needed it, and it means so much to me now that she does. Lord, I've heard of so many people who've really struggled even to find a room in a nursing facility anywhere in our town, getting put on waiting lists and moving around from one place to another . . . Yet, Lord, you blessed us by opening the room here to Mom on the very day she needed it. I don't know what to say or how to say it, but thank you, God, thank you . . .

"I know it won't be easy and I know Mom and I still have many challenges ahead, but I have never before felt surrounded by your peace and presence the way I do right now, Father. So again, let me just thank you, and gratefully and humbly, in the name of your Son, Jesus Christ, ask for your continued mercy and blessings for my mom . . . Amen."

As she finished praying, Meg remained silent, simply experiencing the Father's loving embrace. The tears finally stopped and she gradually became aware once again of the springtime sounds around her—birds singing in a high tree, some ducks fussing along the far shoreline of the pond, and the distant sound of someone's lawn mower. Maybe, she thought, it was even her own teenage son mowing their grass just a few blocks away.

Biblical Insights

Honor your father and your mother, so that you may live long in the land the LORD *your God is giving you.—Exodus 20:12*

You shall not steal.—Exodus 20:15

Honor your father and your mother, as the LORD *your God has commanded you.—Deuteronomy 5:16*

Rise in the presence of the aged, show respect for the elderly and revere your God. I am the LORD.—Leviticus 19:32

Do not cast me away when I am old; do not forsake me when my strength is gone.—Psalm 71:9

Practical Counsel

A blessing of all the medical advances we enjoy is that many of us are living longer lives. But one consequence of these longer lives is that more of us will likely require skilled assistance with our daily activities and health care needs at some point, services often provided in the setting of a long-term care facility. And the cost of such care, as many of us are aware, can be astronomical, very quickly dissipating the modest life savings of all but the wealthiest among us.

Medicaid (sometimes called Medical Assistance) is a federally conceived government welfare program implemented by each state for the purpose of providing access to health care, including skilled nursing care, to people who can't otherwise afford it. (To avoid possible confusion, please note Medicaid is a totally different program from Medicare, which is a federal medical insurance program designed to assist the elderly from all walks of life.) In recent years, an entire cottage industry of lawyers and other "elder care planners" or "Medicaid planners" have sprung up, for the purpose of advising older folks (often quite wealthy older folks) on how to arrange their affairs so as to qualify as "indigent" persons eligible for the benefits of the Medicaid program.

Without regard to life expectancy, material wealth, or available government programs, it seems abundantly clear from the Bible and Christian tradition that God wants us to honor our parents and our elders. It is one of our great privileges and historic responsibilities to care for those older than we are and to look out for their best interests, as their minds and bodies grow weak.

But many secular attorneys and planning professionals (as well as some Christians) seem to embrace a radically different view, essentially asserting we are no longer responsible for taking care of our elderly parents, because "the government" will! This attitude is rooted in concepts of legal liability, rather than of moral obligation. A mentality of entitlement is promoted. Seductive arguments are raised that, since we all pay taxes, there is nothing wrong with doing whatever it takes to qualify our parents for medical assistance from the government. We're simply taking back a piece of what we've already paid in. And we're merely protecting our assets, like any sensible person would (or even like any good steward would). And, after all, the medical assistance planners argue, isn't it better the children enjoy the accumulated wealth of the parents, rather than the parents spending it on nursing home care? Any expectations that the children should bear the burden of caring for elderly relatives are dismissed as quaint, old-fashioned notions from a simpler day, when people actually cared for their own loved ones.

As a Christian, I am forced to conclude that intentionally rearranging our parents' assets to impoverish them, so they can qualify for a government welfare program designed for the poorest among us, and so other family members can freely enjoy those assets, doesn't honor our parents. In fact, I would suggest that it actually disgraces them. Likewise, purposefully hiding or failing to disclose assets in order to qualify a parent for Medicaid is deceptive and a form of theft. We need to guard our hearts and remind ourselves of the warnings Jesus gives us against valuing money and material things over the true treasure of loving and serving him.

All too often, in my experience, adult children are the ones pressuring their elderly parents to get involved in aggressive Medicaid planning, sometimes even to the extent that they are actually the ones bringing their elderly parents to the lawyer's office to start the process. And the children generally have one goal in mind: Save "my" inheritance! Different people come around to the issue in different ways, but that's the bottom line question: "What can we do to 'protect' Mom or Dad's assets, so the money doesn't get spent on nursing home costs, so I get 'my' inheritance?" And while some would argue that it's just good stewardship, in many cases it really has nothing to do with stewardship and everything to do with greed. After all, whose money is it we're talking about here? Mom and Dad's money!

And why have Mom and Dad been saving their money all these years? In most cases, once I talk to Mom and Dad privately, I learn that their primary concern is to make sure they can take care of themselves, so they won't be a burden to their children or anyone else (including the government!). They are embarrassed about even having come to the office to discuss Medicaid planning, but have done so, reluctantly, under intense pressure from their children (or frequently one particular child). And the last thing Mom and Dad want is to end up on any type of welfare program.

Mom and Dad are often deeply uncomfortable about implementing a Medicaid qualification strategy, while the children are often extremely eager for them to start it as soon as possible. Because when Mom or Dad starts to "plan" for the nursing home, most frequently that "planning" really means Mom or Dad must start giving away most of their hard-earned savings to the children *now*. Of course, in planning for Medicaid eligibility, there are many complexities, loopholes, and "look-back periods," but when you move beyond all the fancy jargon and bells and whistles, most nursing home planning in the secular legal community comes down to advising Mom or Dad how to give away assets as rapidly as they can, so they can sooner satisfy the Medicaid program's tests for impoverishment.

Remember, Medicaid is a nice, friendly sounding name for a government welfare program originally intended for the poor and indigent elderly who can't afford medical care. Sadly, the Medicaid welfare program is now being used instead by middle- and higher-income people it was never intended to serve, people who have purposely transferred the bulk of their assets to their children just so they could qualify for Medicaid. So while Mom and Dad go on the public dole, the kids can build a bigger house or go on vacation or whatever. And we all end up paying for it through higher taxes. Putting Mom or Dad on welfare while the kids spend their money may be perfectly legal, but to me it sure looks like a violation of God's commandment to honor your father and your mother.

So, is it wrong to take steps to plan for nursing home care, to try to save money? No, certainly it's wise to plan for the potential expenses of nursing home care, and there are some planning tools that make good moral and financial sense. For example, a high-quality long-term care insurance policy can be an excellent part of good, sound planning, as can investing in home improvements that make home care a viable option for a longer period. And certainly there is nothing morally wrong or inappropriate about a person of limited economic means who genuinely meets the criteria of the Medicaid program taking full advantage of it. But when planning for nursing home care consists of convincing Mom and Dad to transfer most of their assets to their kids, well, then I think it is wrong.

The Bible teaches we are to provide for our own, that we are to honor our fathers and mothers. The world teaches that the smart thing to do is let our fathers and mothers go on government welfare. There is a clear choice to make. It's not always easy being a Christian. Sometimes the things we need to do to honor our faith don't make sense from the world's perspective. But if we can change our focus from the world's perspective to God's perspective, I trust that God will honor our decisions to honor him.

CHAPTER 8

The Living-Will Slippery Slope

Your eyes saw my unformed body. All the days ordained for me
were written in your book before one of them came to be.

—PSALM 139:16

Life Lessons—Reggie and Ruth

"Does this guy have a living will?" the paramedic asked his partner. When his partner shrugged his shoulders, they both looked
expectantly at Ruth. Ruth was flushed with the fear and emotion
of the rushing events of the last twenty minutes—the sudden col-
lapse of her husband, Reggie, the frantic emergency call, the dread
as she cradled his nearly lifeless body in her trembling arms, the
sense of reassurance as the wailing siren of the ambulance finally
reached their driveway. Now she was bewildered. The paramedics
had worked quickly, energetically in the first moments, but now
there was a troubling lack of urgency in their motion. The tone of
the paramedic's question sounded almost impatient.

"Does it matter?" Ruth finally managed.

"Well," responded the paramedic, "it's not looking so good—he's probably been unconscious for almost half an hour, and that's a long time for a brain to be without a good oxygen supply. I was just thinking, if he has a living will, he might be better off if we . . ."

"If we what?" Ruth snapped back, incredulous, "if we let him die right here, right now? That's not gonna happen! Reggie and I have been through too much together—he's always been a fighter, and I'm not gonna let him go just like that! C'mon, you've got to get him to the hospital!"

Later that evening at the medical center, in the cardiac care unit where Reggie now lay unconscious, breathing with the assistance of a ventilator, the attending physician pulled Ruth aside. "Mrs. Reese," she began, diplomatically, "your husband appears to have experienced a lengthy period of oxygen deprivation. He has more than likely suffered severe brain damage. And, of course, his heart is severely compromised. Another cardiac episode could occur at any moment."

The doctor paused, and then continued, lowering her voice as if confiding a secret, "Mrs. Reese, I note from the admission chart that your husband has a valid living will, and that you are his designated surrogate, the one to make medical treatment decisions for him. Quite frankly, Mrs. Reese, if I were in your shoes, I would consider discontinuing the ventilator right now, letting him pass with dignity tonight, before you put him through any more discomfort and before you waste your children's inheritance on unnecessary medical bills."

Ruth was stunned. She very clearly remembered how her attorney had carefully explained that the purpose of the living wills she and Reggie signed a few years back was only to prevent either of their lives from being unduly prolonged in the event of a long-term terminal condition involving permanent unconsciousness and no realistic hope of recovery. *It hasn't even been eight hours since the heart attack,* she thought to herself. *It's much too soon to even con-*

sider using that living will—that's something for down the road, if Reggie gets worse and things become truly hopeless.

Ruth gathered herself and replied to the doctor's recommendation, "Doctor, I'm sorry, I don't know what you're talking about, but I can tell you this—when I was in there with Reggie, he was squeezing my hand . . . and . . . and, I swear I could even see a little smile around his eyes, whenever I would talk to him—Doctor, there's no way I'm gonna let him go until God takes him."

"Oh, well," the doctor sighed as she turned to continue her rounds, "I thought I might be able to save you and your family a lot of unpleasantness and expense, but let me leave you with one thought, Mrs. Reese. Right now, in the condition your husband's in, it's not God's decision whether he lives or dies, it's yours. And the most merciful thing you can do, considering the poor quality of life he'll have even if he does come through all this, might just be to let him die with dignity."

It was two days later when, to the surprise of everyone, Reggie suddenly regained consciousness. No one could explain it with certainty, but the medical consensus was that the oxygen deprivation hadn't been as extended or severe as they had assumed. Communication wasn't easy with all the respiratory tubes and equipment, but soon Reggie and Ruth had worked out a basic system of blinks and hand squeezes. And before long, Ruth decoded one of his very first messages, "I L-O-V-E Y-O-U R-U-T-H." She was overjoyed. She told her friends and family, "Reggie's still in there, and he's fighting to live!" That afternoon, the Reeses' son, still in uniform, finally arrived at the medical center, having been granted emergency leave from his overseas military duty. "W-E-L-C-O-M-E H-O-M-E S-O-N," Reggie quickly signaled, "S-A-L-U-T-E T-O Y-O-U."

Very late that night, after Ruth and her son had gone home for some much-needed sleep, the monitors in Reggie's room suddenly began to flash and blare. The second cardiac episode the physician had anticipated was happening. Reggie's heart had stopped. The night shift staff immediately sprang into action, under the leadership of the young second-year resident physician on duty. But as the young doctor rapidly scanned Reggie's chart, two words caught his eyes—"Living Will"—and his thoughts raced back to fuzzy recollections from the medical ethics and patients' rights course he had struggled to pass in medical school. "Hold it, hold it!" he shouted. "We need to let him go!"

And at his order, the nurses all withdrew, most of them speedily moving on to attend to other patients with their own urgent needs. Within moments, it was over and Reggie's lifeless body was being transported to the hospital morgue. The young doctor's shift was about to end, so he quickly jotted a few final notes of medical jargon in Reggie's chart, knowing the attending physician would soon be back on duty, bearing the burden of explaining things to the family.

And, based on those notes, all Ruth and her son would ever end up being told about Reggie's death is that attempts to resuscitate him had been abandoned. They naturally assumed that this was after some sustained effort at resuscitation had proved unsuccessful—they had no reason to suspect otherwise. But what they would never learn is that the young doctor, either in the confusion of the moment or in his fundamental misunderstanding of the purpose of a living will, had treated Reggie as if a standing "Do Not Resuscitate" order was noted on his chart, and, in the process, had very likely spread his confusion to the staff he was supervising as well.[*]

---

[*] *I apologize in advance to the many fine and well-informed paramedics, nurses, and doctors who fully and clearly understand the proper function of living wills; I do not wish to malign your valiant service, and I thank you sincerely and deeply for that service. However, because I have learned anecdotally of several real-life incidents in which patients with living wills were erroneously treated by medical personnel as if they were the subject of "Do Not Resuscitate" orders (or in which patients actually expected and desired to be treated in that manner and were not!), I am compelled to include these scenarios as a warning and learning tool for patients and medical personnel alike.*

More Life Lessons—The Ming Family

The gentle candlelight and peaceful trickling of clear water through the stones of the small fountain were a welcome relief from the overwhelming brightness and busyness of the rest of the hospital. And as she knelt on a soft cushion to pray, Marisa Ming was grateful her family's pastor had encouraged her to take some time here in the little chapel to reflect and be alone with God. Already, her spirit was awash with a sense of comfort and clarity of direction, a sense of deep understanding and assurance. "Yes," she whispered quietly, "it's time."

Marisa had experienced every imaginable emotion in the weeks since her husband's accident. Hope, denial, anger, grief, more hope, disappointment, and now, finally, resignation and acceptance. The situation was clear. She had received second and third opinions from the best neurology specialists in the region. She had talked to God like never before and read Scripture passage after Scripture passage. She had poured out her heart before her pastor, her children, and her church family. Intercessors had bathed her husband in almost constant streams of prayer. And she would miss him terribly. "But, yes," she again prayed softly, "it's time."

Marco and Marisa had talked about these things over the years. And when they visited their lawyer to make wills, way back when the kids were small, he advised them to put their thoughts in writing, so there wouldn't be any doubt and confusion if ever that time came. "Living wills," he called the written declarations.

And, she remembered, Marco was especially clear about what he wanted: "If I'm ever to the point where there's no hope, where the doctors agree that my brain is no longer working and I'll never get better, well, then, if the only thing keeping my body alive is some machine, then please go ahead and pull the plug. You don't have to be in any rush, but when you're ready, when you've prayed and you're at peace, well, Honey, you know what I want, and you know where I'm going." Marisa could almost hear Marco's voice repeating those words as she glanced down at his signature on the paper she held in her hand, the living will.

"Okay, Marco," she whispered, "okay."

As Marisa emerged from the chapel, her children, who had been huddled in the hospital lobby, quickly came to her side, along with their pastor. She didn't speak a word to any of them, but when she nodded her head, they knew. And with her son's arm around her shoulder in strong support and her daughter firmly grasping her hand, together they walked slowly toward the intensive care unit, where Marco and his doctor patiently awaited her decision.

Biblical Insights

You shall not murder.—Exodus 20:13

Rise in the presence of the aged, show respect for the elderly and revere your God. I am the LORD.—Leviticus 19:32

Do not cast me away when I am old; do not forsake me when my strength is gone.—Psalm 71:9

Yet I am always with you; you hold me by my right hand. You guide me with your counsel, and afterward you will take me into glory. —Psalm 73:23–24

As a father has compassion on his children, so the LORD has compassion on those who fear him; for he knows how we are formed, he remembers that we are dust. As for man, his days are like grass, he flourishes like a flower of the field; the wind blows over it and it is gone, and its place remembers it no more. But from everlasting to everlasting the LORD's love is with those who fear him, and his righteousness with their children's children—with those who keep his covenant and remember to obey his precepts.—Psalm 103:13–18

Practical Counsel

Living wills (unlike living trusts, discussed in chapter 6) are documents specifically designed to express our wishes and desires for health care treatment in the event we can no longer communicate for ourselves *and* we have deteriorated into a terminal condition of permanent unconsciousness (often referred to as a "persistent vegetative state"). Sometimes, you will hear living wills called "advance directives," and the terms are synonymous.

Each state has its own laws about living wills, so some of the particulars will vary from state to state, such as exactly how we are to define "permanent unconsciousness." Now and then, certain court cases make headlines as families and other interested parties wrangle over the precise meanings of some of the key terms. But, as a whole, living wills are quite commonly utilized, usually without incident or dispute.

Before addressing the concerns I have as a Christian attorney with respect to living wills and their uses and possible misuses, let me very quickly discuss the background of how the living will arose. As medical science advanced in the last century, our society experienced a new phenomenon for the first time—individuals with normally fatal injuries and illnesses could sometimes be kept physically alive with the assistance of technology. But if the technology were removed or withdrawn, these individuals would quickly die.

In most instances, the new medical technology was a very good thing. Accident victims could be kept alive until their injuries healed. Victims of certain illnesses, such as kidney disease, could lead years and years of productive life by relying on machines to perform the functions that would ordinarily have been performed by their now-damaged organs. The list goes on and on.

But in some cases, usually where the individual in question had suffered some type of severe brain damage, a new ethical problem arose. What if medical technology could keep a person's body alive indefinitely? What if that person's brain was no longer capable of the functions associated with living or "consciousness"? Now what? Was the person really alive? Was the person actually dead, even though many parts of his or her body were still functioning? Who would have the right to define the meaning of the new term *brain dead*?

The living will arose as a way to address some of these issues. Over the period of a decade or so, most states adopted a living-will statute, including definitions of the relevant terms, subject, of course, to further interpretation by the courts. The typical living-will law enables individuals to create legally binding written expressions of their wishes, to be relied upon in the event they should ever slip into an unconscious condition from which no significant recovery is deemed realistically possible by the appropriate medical professionals. Often the living will includes the appointment of a surrogate, or agent, to serve as an advocate for the implementation of the preferences of the unconscious person, as expressed in the written document.

Most living wills request that all further life-sustaining treatment be withdrawn in the event of terminal, permanent unconsciousness. Many also include provisions that medications to keep the unconscious person "comfortable" and free from severe pain should continue to be administered, despite the cessation of other treatments. Obviously, the direct result of following the instructions set forth in most living wills is clinical death of the patient.

Now, the reason I felt it necessary to include a chapter in this book on living wills is not so much the typical situation described above, although as a believer in God's ultimate sovereignty I do have some personal misgivings about even standard living wills (as of this writing, I do not have a living will in force for myself). However, I would be the first to admit that thoughtful Christians hold very diverse views on this subject, and that many denominations and individual churches have studied these issues at great length, many concluding that the standard living-will concept is entirely acceptable from the perspective of Scripture and Christian ethics.

My fundamental concern about living wills arises not from their use as initially envisioned, but rather from the common misuse, misapplication, and misunderstanding of the living-will concept. I believe that God views human life as a sacred thing. However, there are many groups and individuals within our culture who do not share that view. These forces manifest themselves in various ways at various times. Sometimes they act very publicly and boldly, such as through the infamous "assisted suicides" of Dr. Kevorkian or through embracing the horrific practices of partial-birth abortion. But sometimes they act very quietly and subtly. And because, on the surface at least, the living will sounds so reasonable, so innocuous, so acceptable, I believe that those who would actively promote an agenda of death have co-opted the living-will concept to cloak themselves in respectability, as they continue to work to undermine the traditional Christian view of human life as a sacred thing.

Here is what I have observed over my years of practice. This is not based on any empirical study, just my observation. I sense there has been a general shift in perception, such that rather than the living will being viewed as something to be thoughtfully, prayerfully, and reluctantly relied upon only after the passage of substantial time and extensive review and consultation with attending physicians, other medical personnel, and loved ones, I now see the living will being viewed as something that should be acted upon in extreme haste, in the very heat of the onset of a medical crisis, before anyone can really discern how permanent or lasting the condition in question will be. I observe this troubling attitude manifested in clients who ask about carrying their living wills on their person "in case we get in an accident;" I observe it manifested in any number of stories I've heard of medical personnel (from doctors and nurses to ambulance crews) treating patients with living wills in the same manner as they would a patient with a "Do Not Resuscitate" order on the medical chart; and I observe it manifested in the popular press, where reporters seem to perpetuate these misconceptions about the proper purpose of the living will.

Quite frankly, I believe something dangerous is happening with respect to the way living wills are coming to be understood by our society at large, something that is moving our culture closer to openly embracing euthanasia, or "mercy killing," for anyone who can't speak for themselves (even temporarily) and who appears to have poor prospects for resuming a high "quality of life" after an illness or injury.

So here are some considerations for a Christian who prefers to trust in God's timing, rather than in the timing of someone who can't or won't distinguish between a living will and a "Do Not Resuscitate" order. First, you should be aware that although hospitals are generally required to inquire as to whether you have a living will, that does not mean you must have one to be admitted! They simply have to ask. But you aren't required to answer "Yes"!

Second, you should be aware you can actually make a legally binding, written advance directive that states the very opposite of most living wills. In other words, you can specify your desire for all available health care treatment to be provided to you, no matter what your condition, and your overall preference for life under all circumstances. Secular attorneys may not be familiar with these unique types of advance directives, but many Christian attorneys should be. (If your attorney is not, then please refer them to the resource Appendix at the end of this book to find out more about these "Wills to Live").

And, lastly, in the midst of any pressure, confusion, or doubt you may experience in wrestling with these end-of-life issues, please do not forget that each of us is a precious child of the King of the universe, a treasure to him of inestimable worth, and that his timing is perfect!

CHAPTER 9

The Bankruptcy Bailout

"Everything is permissible"—but not everything is beneficial.
"Everything is permissible"—but not everything is constructive.
Nobody should seek his own good, but the good of others.

—1 CORINTHIANS 10:23–24

Life Lessons—Lenny and Lynn

"Keep your head down," Lenny whispered urgently to Lynn. "It's Quinn! Don't let him see us!"

Silently Lynn bowed her head, her skin flushing with embarrassment as she and Lenny tried to melt into the line of people waiting to be seated for dinner. She knew the drill all too well. Ever since Lenny's business venture had gone under, it seemed like everywhere they went they ran into people who had lent money to Lenny. Tonight at the restaurant, it was the same. And even if Quinn didn't spot them, dinner would be tense. But at least that was better than another loud public confrontation with

Quinn, who always saw to it that everyone within earshot was made fully aware that Lenny had "welched" on the $50,000 he'd borrowed.

Tonight, they were fortunate. Quinn never did spot them. But on the drive home, Lenny noticed Lynn was weeping. "What's wrong, Honey?" Lenny asked, already suspecting the answer.

"I just can't take this anymore, Lenny," Lynn stammered, "I feel like such a lowlife. This is a small town and everyone knows about us. And everywhere we go, we seem to run into one of those guys you convinced to loan you money. I just can't go on knowing we aren't even trying to pay them back."

"Hey now, Lynn," Lenny began reflexively, in an almost lecturing tone, "we've had this conversation before. You know the bankruptcy is over and we don't legally owe those guys a dime, not a dime. It's their problem now—they knew there was risk involved; they aren't stupid. Like our lawyer says, they'll just have to get used to it. They don't have a thing on us. The bankruptcy judge took care of all that."

"But, Lenny, you know as well as I do that those guys didn't pitch in with the loans thinking about business and risk," Lynn retorted, "they did it because they liked you and thought you were a man of integrity—you promised them, you looked them in the eye and said you would make sure they got every penny back. And now look at us, ducking around in restaurants like a couple of fugitives—and, honestly, I don't even feel right about us eating at these fancy places, driving this nice car, none of it, not when those guys are out all that money."

"Oh, come on, Lynn," Lenny began mocking, "you're not gonna start on one of your super-morality kicks again—'do unto others' and all that—because I'll tell you what, the law's the law, and the law says we don't owe the money. And that's good enough for me. That's exactly why I hired a lawyer, and he did his job well. Now let's drop it."

But Lynn wasn't finished. "Did you ever stop to think, Len," she continued firmly, "did you ever stop to think about where you met that young Dave Delmuto, you know, the one who lent you the last $10,000, right before the end?" Lynn instantly answered her own question before Lenny had a chance to speak. "It was at church, Len. And you might remember that the Delmuto family was new in town. But did you know they had never been involved with a church before? Did you know that Dave and his wife were new believers? And did you notice they haven't been back in church since the week your lawyer sent out those letters to all the people you owed money to, telling them about the bankruptcy? Can't you put two and two together?"

Lenny was now starting to breathe heavily, a mixture of anger and guilt slowly building in his heart. Lynn didn't let up. "Do you realize what you're doing, Lenny? Well, let me spell it out for you. You've turned your wife into an outsider in her own hometown. Do you know how many of my friends won't even talk to me anymore? You've embarrassed your kids, made them ashamed to have you as a dad. Do you realize the way the other kids torment them at school? You've alienated some of your oldest friends, and you don't even seem to care. And, worst of all, I'm pretty sure your actions drove Dave Delmuto and his wife and his kids away from the Lord—who knows, maybe for eternity. Don't you get it? As a man who calls himself a Christian, your conduct, your witness in this community, your refusal to take responsibility for your mistakes . . . Lenny, you're dishonoring Jesus Christ. I don't know how else to say it."

Lenny and Lynn were silent for the rest of the drive home. Lenny was obviously thinking, but Lynn had no idea if her bold speech had made an impact. When they pulled into the garage, Lenny sat motionless behind the wheel, a faraway expression on his face, still not saying a word. Hoping he finally understood the damage he had done and just needed some time alone to work through his thoughts, Lynn quickly went inside the house to check on the kids, finding them upstairs doing homework as promised.

After spending a few minutes with the kids, Lynn gathered some laundry in a basket and headed downstairs for the washer. But as she entered the laundry room near the garage, a smoky smell made her cough and she heard an engine running. In a horrified instant her heart began to pound and she dropped the laundry basket, yanking open the door to the garage to investigate.

Through a haze of choking exhaust fumes, she saw Lenny, slumped in the car. Reflexively, she pushed the garage door opener button mounted beside the doorway and scrambled to open the car and shut off the ignition. Thankfully, Lenny hadn't locked the doors and he was still breathing and semi-conscious as Lynn desperately dragged him from the car toward the fresh air now rushing in from outside.

With Lenny on the ground gasping, Lynn's trembling hands made the emergency call on her cell phone and soon an ambulance was on the scene. By now the kids had heard the commotion and stood hugging their shaken mother. The paramedics were filling Lenny's lungs with oxygen and one of them, reassuring the terrified family, explained. "You found him just in time. He hadn't been in there too long yet and I think he's going to be okay."

Just then, glancing down through misty eyes, Lynn noticed a crumpled piece of paper on the garage floor. She leaned over to pick it up and recognized Lenny's writing. It must have fallen from his hand as she dragged him across the floor. On it were two words, "I'm sorry."

More Life Lessons—Jason and Jan

Getting into debt was the easy part. The hard part was digging out. But now, three years of discipline and hard work had finally paid off, and Jason and Jan sat on the balcony of their small apartment and reminisced. "What would you say was your lowest moment?" Jason asked, as they watched the summer sun dropping slowly beyond the distant mountains west of town.

"I'm thinking of the day we went to see that bankruptcy lawyer," Jan said wistfully. "Things were getting so bad, all the phone calls from the credit card companies, the money we borrowed from your brother—remember how we didn't have the heart to tell him it was all gone? Anyway, that day at the lawyer's office was so depressing, how we couldn't even scrape up the fee he needed to start our bankruptcy filing! We were too poor to go bankrupt! I was never so embarrassed in my life! And everything seemed so hopeless—honestly, I didn't even know if you and I could stick it out together, things were getting so tense between us."

"Yeah," chuckled Jason, "but we can laugh about it now. I think of that day every time I see one of those big ugly 'Get Rid of Bills—Get Rid of Bill Collectors' billboards that that lawyer still has around town. But I'm so glad we didn't have the money. Who knows how far gone we'd be today if we hadn't gotten help with our real problem? Bankruptcy would have been a Band-Aid, but we needed a cure, not more excuses.

"Okay, what was your best moment, the most satisfying?" Jason now inquired.

"I think it's a tie," Jan offered. "First, there was that afternoon, a couple days after we got kicked out of the lawyer's office, the afternoon we went down to the church with our bright idea of seeing if they would help us with the money we needed for the bankruptcy filing fees. I can't believe we had the nerve to expect it, but we were so wrapped up in everything, and so naive. But Pastor Rob was smooth, so quick to recognize what we really needed, and he told us he'd consider helping us with the money if we would spend three sessions of Christian financial counseling with him first. We were impatient, but we figured we didn't have any better prospects of getting the cash we needed.

"Well, it was that first session with Pastor Rob that I still treasure, when we finally understood the concept of stewardship for the first time. How God owns it all and we're just caretakers, and the way the Holy Spirit moved in our hearts that day to help us grasp the vision for the joy and simplicity of living within our means. That day changed everything—and, of course, by the time we completed that first counseling session, we realized we didn't want or need to file bankruptcy, we just needed to make a plan and stick to it, with God's help."

"Amen to that!" shouted Jason. "And we did it!" Then, with his fist still raised triumphantly, he asked, "Okay, and what's your other one, the other best moment?"

"You know," Jan said, "this might sound odd, but the other best moment was the day we went to your brother's place and confessed we'd squandered all the money he lent us. He was so calm, so merciful, so loving. And I was so thankful when he offered us the chance to make it up by working for him down at the café. All those months of long nights closing up the place—sweeping and mopping, scrubbing the bathrooms, and hauling the trash—it was brutal, after working our regular jobs all day.

"But you know what? It was just so satisfying to be able to work our way out of the hole we were in with him in a way that really helped him. And it was the best thing that could have happened to you and me, because we really got to spend some quality time together, just the two of us with nothing to do but talk and work our butts off. We really needed that, and our relationship has been so much stronger ever since."

"Yes, God is good!" exclaimed Jason, "and his ways are above our ways—that's for sure! Who would have guessed financial ruin could be turned into a blessing? And man, that old Devil must be so frustrated about the way this turned out!"

Jan thought for a moment, then added, "Just think, right now those last three checks are on some mail truck somewhere, and by morning they'll be delivered and cashed. I know it's kind of corny—I know they're big credit card companies and companies don't have souls—but I prayed over those checks today before I mailed them, asking God to bless whoever handles them, and thanking God for the way those big companies worked with us at the beginning, to get us on a payment schedule we could manage. They didn't have to do that, but I'm so thankful they did. And I thanked God for allowing us to hold up our end of the deal."

Jason was nodding. "Amen again!" he said enthusiastically. "And now, Jan, I'll always picture you praying over the mail whenever I see one of those goofy 'Get Rid of Bills—Get Rid of Bill Collectors' signs, because your way is the right way!"

Biblical Insights

The wicked borrow and do not repay, but the righteous give generously.
—Psalm 37:21

Let no debt remain outstanding, except the continuing debt to love one another, for he who loves his fellowman has fulfilled the law.
—Romans 13:8

Practical Counsel

Bankruptcy is a federally supervised legal process designed to provide a fresh financial start for honest debtors, people who owe more than they can realistically repay. At the conclusion of a standard bankruptcy, the court issues a discharge, essentially wiping the debtor's slate clean. Creditors (those who are owed money) must simply accept whatever payment, if any, the court requires the debtor to pay, take their losses on the rest, and move on.

The concept behind bankruptcy is honorable and merciful, and inherently biblical as well, with roots in the Old Testament "year of jubilee," when debts would be periodically forgiven. Before bankruptcy laws were adopted, the bleak alternatives available to those who had overstepped their economic means were often involuntary servitude or debtors' prison. So bankruptcy laws were essentially a measure of reform in our society, something Christians could celebrate and endorse.

But, like so many of our cherished freedoms, the bankruptcy concept was intended for a culture in which strong Christian moral values were prevalent. Whether a person could legally qualify for bankruptcy protection or not, it was generally understood that bankruptcy would be used by debtors only as a last resort. Today, however, in our emerging post-Christian culture, those assumptions no longer hold true.

Now, declaring bankruptcy has become a common and acceptable alternative for folks who find themselves financially overextended, even to a fairly modest degree. Some even intentionally overspend and abusively max out all available credit, secure in the knowledge bankruptcy will provide them with a quick fix at the end of their spree. The prevailing attitude seems to be "if it's legal, it must be okay."

Many perceive bankruptcy as nothing more than a great way to start over, with very few strings attached. Others turn to bankruptcy because their debts are so overwhelming they feel they have no realistic choice. And others see bankruptcy as an opportunity to turn the tables and take advantage of big "greedy" financial institutions and credit card companies, who obviously should have known better than to lend so much money. All in all, bankruptcy seems to have developed into just another option, a personal decision to be made without regard for how it affects anyone else. And many attorneys are more than happy to oblige their clients in pursuing the bankruptcy process, sometimes even actively promoting and encouraging the bankruptcy option.

But the Bible admonishes Christians to repay what we owe. And Scripture specifically calls us to consider the benefit of others rather than focusing on ourselves. Bankruptcy, however, allows us to avoid repaying what we owe and denies others something that is rightfully theirs, which is seldom to their benefit. And, as Christians, how effective will our witness be to people we've promised to pay when we later fail to keep our word, simply walking away from our obligations? Failure to pay our debts can damage our relationships by inspiring mistrust and resentment, in direct contradiction to Jesus' call to treat others as we would want to be treated. A follower of Christ, even if legally released from debt by bankruptcy, still remains morally obligated to repay what is owed.

Many people, including Christians, struggle financially, trying to keep up with car payments, credit card bills, and other expenses. Certainly, some folks can end up in real trouble when they've gotten in over their heads. So what can a Christian in this situation do? Are there morally acceptable legal options? As Christians, we should first embrace options that enable us to make sure those who have loaned us money get paid back (even the big credit card companies and financial institutions!). We need to remember we answer to God, and God's Word tells us to repay what we owe. But what if it's too much? What if there's too much month left at the end of our money?

In most cases, the fundamental action step is to talk to creditors early and often, with the more communication the better. Let creditors know you have every intention of repaying, that you haven't forgotten about them. Of course, not every creditor will be interested in discussing a past-due debt, but many creditors are willing to listen and perhaps even renegotiate terms to make repayment realistic. A typical creditor would rather receive smaller on-time payments than face the prospect of a totally delinquent account.

If the situation is dire and your creditors won't listen, or won't take action to lower the payments or otherwise renegotiate the terms of the debt, then the next best thing for a Christian is often to get in touch with a nonprofit credit counseling service, preferably one with a Christian perspective. Legitimate credit counseling services tend to have incredible clout with credit card and finance companies. They can frequently help Christians in trouble to avoid bankruptcy by negotiating a restructuring of debt terms, so the Christian can honor God's instruction to repay, without falling into a financial and legal black hole. However, you should research your credit counseling service carefully before signing up, as there have been persistent instances of consumer fraud and scam operations in the credit counseling field.

But what if even a good credit counseling service can't get the creditors to compromise? Is bankruptcy an option for a Christian in financial trouble? Can bankruptcy fit in with God's plan for a Christian?

Yes, bankruptcy is an option for Christians. But I would suggest that a Christian evaluating the possibility of bankruptcy should first prayerfully consider the pain it might cause those on the other side—the people who have been counting on being repaid. There's a real moral issue. Just because bankruptcy is legal doesn't mean a Christian should go that route. To me, the bottom line is "Are the creditors going to get paid back?" If the events in a person's life spin out of control, they've prayed about it, asked the church family for help, done everything they can, but still there's no way out, then I'm aware of nothing in the Scriptures that prohibits bankruptcy. But even then, I believe the person should make every effort to repay the debts, even if it ends up being years after the bankruptcy is concluded. The legal discharge of debts issued by the court in a bankruptcy proceeding never erases our moral obligation to repay those who have been willing to loan us money.

Moving forward in the aftermath of bankruptcy is a circumstance in which being a Christian might be more expensive than being a nonbeliever. More than likely, in the world's eyes, a Christian would be considered a fool to diligently repay his creditors after a bankruptcy. But obeying God's Word brings us blessings the world might never understand. Those blessings might not even happen this side of heaven. But we trust that God will honor those who honor him.

CHAPTER 10

The Business of Ethics

The acquisition of treasures by a lying tongue
is a fleeting vapor, the pursuit of death.

—PROVERBS 21:6

Life Lessons—Kipp Konstruction

"Perfect, beautiful!" Kent Kipp shouted, a proud smile on his face as the crane operator lowered the gleaming new sign atop the towering steel pole.

Kent turned quickly, strode across the sprawling lawn of his new company headquarters building, through the freshly paved parking lot, and around back to the spacious new maintenance shop.

Noticing one of his supply trucks still in the shop, Kent's countenance quickly changed. "What did I tell you??? Get that truck on the road now, you moron, or you're fired!" he barked angrily, grabbing the front of the chief mechanic's shirt for emphasis.

"Mr. Kipp," the mechanic stammered, "that axle could go any time—someone could get killed if it happens on the road—the parts are on the way—I could have it done by . . ."

Kent cut him off before he could finish, "It's done right now. Tell the driver it's done. Or you're done. Understand? I got twenty men out on the Depot job right now standing around waiting for those loads of roof trusses—I'm paying them to do nothing!!! Do you understand that? Nothing—on my dime!!! It doesn't work that way. The truck is done now, roll it out. Now!" Kent then stood there, glaring at the mechanic until he complied with his order, paging the driver and pulling the truck out of the garage onto the blacktop.

Satisfied his men would soon be back at work, Kent headed over to the office building. Approaching the rear entrance, he noticed the landscaping contractor jogging toward him, waving his hat. *Let's see how good I am today*, Kent thought, smirking to himself.

"Mr. Kipp," the contractor began breathlessly, "it's July and I've been mowing this place almost every week since May, when the sod was put in. Edging, watering, the whole works. I said I'd do this job for the summer, but I'm a one-man shop and I can't afford to keep giving you a full day every week if you don't pay me. You owe me almost $3,500 now and I need the money bad. I've been trying to call you, but my messages don't seem to get through."

"Look, Pal," Kent said slowly, "I'm embarrassed about this. Payroll's eating me alive. I got lots of jobs going, but they're all big ones and nothing's gonna clear until October. Tell you what. If you hang in with me, keep mowing for the rest of the summer, I'll double up when the money starts to come in. Double whatever your bill is. You take care of me, I'll take care of you."

"I'm not so sure I can do that," the contractor replied. "My wife . . ."

Kent saw his opening and jumped. "Your wife! What are you, a little momma's boy? Who calls the shots? Who makes the decisions? You're the man. I just said I'd double your money. If you can't see what a deal you're getting, then I don't even want you cutting my grass. I got guys coming by here every week trying to get this job. Our deal was for the whole summer and you won't see a penny if you break that on me. Nobody walks off the job on Kent Kipp!"

There was an awkward silence as the contractor stared into Kent's eyes for a moment, then looked down. "Double?" the contractor asked sheepishly.

"Double," Kent replied, his eyes now sparkling. He knew he'd won again, and it felt good. Even with the big new lawn, he'd pulled it off. He knew how hungry for work these landscape contractors were, and how many new ones were out there every spring. And now this would be the fourteenth year in a row Kipp Konstruction hadn't paid a cent for lawn mowing and landscaping. Sure, he'd have to pay his lawyer a couple of hundred bucks to scare the guy away in the end, but it worked every time. These landscape guys were small-time and they couldn't afford to fight him for the money. There was nothing in writing. And the line about Kent supposedly promising to double the money was always good for a laugh all around. *Who would be stupid enough to believe that?* Kent chuckled to himself as he walked inside the building.

Settling into his sprawling new office, rocking back in his soft leather chair with his feet up on the big solid wood desk, Kent pondered his next move. The day was still young. Suddenly, his eyes flashed and he barked out loudly, "Hey, Suzie, get in here right now, and bring me that updated jobs-in-progress list—move it, Honey, shake your sugar for the bossman!"

Suzie's concern about her new assignment as executive assistant with Kipp Konstruction had deepened in the few weeks since she'd been hired. As a single mom with two young kids, she knew the advertised money and benefits were awfully good. But now she could see that the above-market salary came with more than a few catches. Not only was she answering half a dozen calls from angry customers and suppliers almost every day, but Kent was gradually making more and more off-color and inappropriate comments to her.

Last week he'd even started making suggestions about her wardrobe. Playing along, hoping to impress Kent and earn his trust, she had reluctantly done some shopping over the weekend. Now she approached Kent's desk hesitantly, feeling extremely self-conscious in her new outfit as Kent brazenly studied her every step.

She placed the list on the corner of the desk with a slightly trembling hand and turned to leave. Grinning, Kent finally spoke. "That's more like it, Suzie—now you're catching on—at Kipp Konstruction, we like to show off our assets, and, Suzie, you've got the assets!" And then, summoning Suzie back over to the desk, he insisted she take a seat in one of the plush office chairs. "Listen, Suzie Baby," he continued, his tone now turning somewhat grave and urgent, "there's more to the benefit package here at Kipp than I told you when you were hired . . . there's ways you can make things work for me and my guys and I can make things work for you, if you know what I mean . . . and come Christmas bonus time, trust me, you'll be glad you did. Why, some years I've had girls bringing in double their regular salary, girls with the right kind of assets, girls like you, Suzie. That kind of money buys a lot of Christmas presents for those kiddos—and that's really what it's all about, isn't it, doing the right thing, taking care of those kids the way they deserve?"

Suzie sat fidgeting, flushed, and embarrassed as Kent went on, now adopting a very warm and reassuring tone. "Suzie, Honey, there's no hurry, no pressure, you just think things over, think about the kids . . . I know you'll do the right thing . . . and I promise, come Christmastime I'll take very good care of you." And with that, Kent winked and snapped playfully. "Now, shake it on out of here, Baby, I've got some calls to make!"

When the door closed behind Suzie, Kent's eyes glanced down over the job list she'd brought him and he casually called his project manager, Jack Jurgenson, on the company intercom system. "Yeah, Jack, I just made sweet Suzie an offer—want to take a bet on how long she holds out?"

Jack's loud laugh pierced Kent's ear. "Kent, you're so smooth I don't give her a week—you didn't use your standard line about the 'double salary' again, did you, Kent? Even I feel bad about that—those young moms you hire just can't walk away from that line—it's like shooting fish in a barrel, too easy."

Kent shook his head as he answered, "Jack, old buddy, let's just say 'business is business' and you've got to stick with the things that work. Now listen, you and I have some real good times coming our way, until we have to let poor Suzie go, so you need to get busy and hold up your end of the deal. I've got the jobs-in-progress list right here—let's see, the Hobson job should be worth at least another $20,000, the new medical building has got to be good for another $40,000 or $50,000, and you can probably squeeze at least another $5,000 from that church job. Heck, J.J., let's look at it this way—you get me the whole $75,000 from those three jobs and Suzie's all yours—exclusive rights!"

Kent laughed out loud to himself as the intercom clicked off. *Exclusive rights!* he thought. *Sometimes I amaze myself! And I think old Jack's buying it—well, he'll never know and I'll make sure little Suzie keeps her mouth shut—what old Jack doesn't know won't hurt him.* Then, tossing the job list into the wastebasket, Kent's mind drifted, imagining the scenes about to unfold on the job sites as Jack skillfully approached the customers with whatever creative excuses he could dream up to explain why the job had unexpectedly gone over the contract price.

Kent envisioned with relish each customer's angry reaction, the heated words, Jack sternly threatening to pull the Kipp Konstruction crew off the job, the breathless phone calls, and then finally the customer's begrudging acceptance of the new price. *I've got this down to a science,* thought Kent. *The key is not demanding too much, but not leaving anything on the table, either—it's that perfect amount—more than they want to pay, but not so much they get their lawyers involved. And the timing is key, just at that spot in the job when it's almost impossible for them to find someone else to come in and finish it without spending a fortune, and right when they're getting really on edge about making the completion date.*

Suzie's voice on the intercom broke Kent's train of thought. She sounded almost distraught. "I'm so sorry, Mr. Kipp, I know you said no phone calls, but this lady is so upset, she's called four or five times already today, she's desperate to get some help—something's gone terribly wrong at the new restaurant we built. The ventilation system is all messed up and smoke from the grills is going everywhere inside—they can't even use the dining room. They had to shut the whole place down—she's in a total panic!"

Kent paused before answering, purposely leaving Suzie in extended silence. Eventually Suzie spoke again. "Mr. Kipp? Are you there, Mr. Kipp?"

Kent finally answered, sounding very annoyed. "Suzie, you know my policy on phone calls. I explained that very clearly on the day you started. We're going to have to get you straightened out—we'll see, but under my office rules I should dock you today's pay for this."

Suzie was exasperated. "I'm so sorry, Mr. Kipp—this lady, the restaurant owner, I just feel so sorry for her, her whole business is shut down. I just thought maybe there was something we could do."

Kent maintained his disgruntled tone. "Suzie, you just get back on the phone with her and tell her, 'It is what it is, we don't give warranties,' and if she doesn't stop calling us, we'll have our lawyers file charges against her for harassment. And Suzie, I want you in my office first thing tomorrow morning so we can work something out on your pay for today—I am very disappointed."

As the conversation ended, Kent once again found himself grinning, mentally patting himself on the back for his ability to intimidate people and put them off balance. *Nope, nobody goes toe-to-toe with Kent Kipp and wins—not my customers, not my employees, nobody—and now I won't even have to wait out the rest of the week for little Suzie—too bad I worked myself into a spot where I can't brag about her to Jack Jurgenson over lunch tomorrow! Promising him that exclusive deal was my only mistake!*

Kent looked at his watch. *Almost time for my meeting with Dr. Cohen, the sucker—I mean,* investor. He stood up, stretched, and looked out the window, where he saw the late-model luxury sedan pull into the lot and park in the spot marked for visitors. Kent headed quickly outside to meet his guest, casting an intimidating glare at Suzie as he passed by her desk.

Kent greeted Dr. Cohen enthusiastically. He knew from their conversation at a recent civic club meeting that Dr. Cohen was new in the area and had substantial sums of money to invest, and Kent had succeeded in interesting him in the growth potential of Kipp Konstruction Inc. Kent knew the brand-new facilities would make a very positive impression and, leaving nothing to chance, he arranged for his accounting clerk to prepare a financial history and a set of glowing projections to match the promising outward appearance of the company.

In the parking lot, Kent and the doctor stood admiring the shiny new sign on the high pole. Dr. Cohen asked Kent about the "fish" symbol covering the lower section of the sign. "Oh, that," replied Kent. "It's the Christian fish—having that little fish on my sign and in my advertising helps the company get lots of construction jobs for churches and charities, and I love those jobs because those people are the easiest to—well, let's just say we get our best profit margin on our church jobs!"

Throughout their tour of the facilities and their inspiring visit to the accounting office, Kent was probing and observing Dr. Cohen, trying to determine his level of sophistication in business and financial matters. By the time they adjourned back to Kent's office, Kent sensed he had Dr. Cohen's mark—a smart man, probably an excellent doctor, but almost no business experience and only the most basic investment knowledge. Kent moved quickly, taking the book of corporate minutes down from its shelf with great ceremony and removing a blank stock certificate. He wrote Dr. Cohen's name on the certificate and indicated the doctor would be the holder of 250 shares, "a substantial minority position in the company." Kent then signed the certificate as president and affixed the corporate seal. "All I need," Kent announced, "is your check for $250,000 and it's a done deal."

Dr. Cohen hesitated for a moment, asking, "Shouldn't there be lawyers involved, or something official like that?" But Kent was on his game and quickly convinced the doctor this was a simple matter and that lawyers would only make things more complicated and much more expensive. "And besides," added Kent earnestly, "my business is built on handshakes and if my handshake isn't good enough for you, then I don't want you as an investor in Kipp Konstruction Inc.—and, trust me, I have others who are interested in purchasing this equity interest in the company if you don't believe in what we're doing here! I only felt obligated to reserve this opportunity for you because we talked about it at the club meeting last month." And with that, Dr. Cohen looked Kent in the eye and wrote out the check, handing it to Kent in exchange for the stock certificate.

And as he hospitably escorted his newest shareholder back to his car in the parking lot, making a mindless stream of investment performance promises all the way, Kent's mind raced with the things the good doctor's lawyer might have warned him about, if only he had been given a chance to scrutinize the transaction. Things like the long history of lawsuits filed by previous shareholders against Kent and the company when they never received their promised returns. And that the company, itself, actually owned none of the impressive buildings and grounds where it was housed, nor any of the equipment or furnishings. Or that the 250 shares purchased represented only a tiny fraction of the 500,000 outstanding shares in the company, and that the company had never paid a single dividend in its entire history. Or that the corporate bylaws made it legally impossible for the doctor to sell his shares to anyone except back to Kent or the company, and then only at a very substantial discount. Or that several layers of bank financing encumbered even the very minimal corporate assets that did exist and tipped the real corporate balance sheets well into the red. Or that the sum paid to Kent in exchange for the stock would more than likely be expended by Kent at his own personal whim and never used to capitalize or operate the company. Or that Kent appeared to be ignoring numerous state and federal rules for securities offerings and tax reporting. But to Kent, all those things were "what ifs"—things a lawyer might have discovered, but that Dr. Cohen would discover only too late. And, Kent thought to himself, *That's just business—you've got to do it to them before they do it to you.*

Dr. Cohen drove off and Kent strolled easily back toward the office building. It was quitting time, and Suzie's silhouette on the sidewalk outside the building quickly caught his eye. She was coming toward him, waving. "Mr. Kipp, I'm so glad I caught you . . . I really want to apologize for that crazy phone call thing earlier today. I know I messed up, and I know it's your policy to dock employees who mess up. You're the boss and that's the way it is, and I understand that . . ."

Kent just stared blankly, listening as if barely interested in the words being spoken. Suzie looked uncomfortable, like she might start crying, but she composed herself and continued, with a suddenly detached but determined look in her eyes. "Mr. Kipp, I think I get the picture . . . you know how bad I need this job . . . I'm so far behind with all my bills and my rent . . . and the kids, well, you know what that's like, I can hardly keep up and they don't get what they deserve. So, so . . . I guess I was wondering if it might be helpful . . . maybe if that's the right word . . . helpful if I could get here say, maybe extra early, like maybe an hour early or something tomorrow . . . to meet with you in your office to, you know . . . go over things, maybe smooth things out, try to make up for how I messed up. Would that be . . . helpful . . . helpful to you?"

Again, Kent stared blankly, then tersely responded, "Could be."

Suzie, still seemingly unsteady but determined, replied, "Thank you, Mr. Kipp. I mean thank you for listening. You won't regret it. I think everything will be okay. I'll be there. I'll see you then. Thank you." Suzie turned and walked to her car.

Kent continued back inside, raising his fist victoriously as soon as he was sure he was out of sight, and exclaiming into the empty hallway, "What a roll I'm on today! And it only gets better tomorrow!"

By the time Kent reached his office, he realized his conversation with Suzie had him running later than usual. As he called his wife at home to tell her he'd be late for dinner, he noticed some police cars pulling into his parking lot. *Wonder what that's about?* he thought absently, as he mumbled some excuses into the phone about why he was delayed. But the next thing he knew, there was violent pounding on the doors at the end of the hall, and the sound of breaking glass and shouting.

"What in the world?" Kent demanded loudly, as five or six heavily armed police officers stormed into his office and pinned him to the floor. In the confusion, Kent heard words like *warrant* and *arrest* and something about his right to have an attorney.

Within minutes, dozens of police and men in suits were swarming everywhere, rifling through files, grabbing computers, everything they could get their hands on. Kent watched, in shock, as he was cuffed, dragged through the corridor, and taken outside into one of the police cars, which then sped away.

It was hours until Kent was finally able to talk with his attorney at the jail holding center, and the meeting wasn't a happy one. The attorney explained Kent was the subject of a joint federal and state investigation, and that he was facing multiple felony charges for securities fraud, tax evasion, and racketeering. Plus several other agencies were looking into charges and civil actions for workplace safety violations, sexual harassment, unfair and deceptive trade practices, and payroll irregularities.

"And," the attorney added, "to make matters worse, a few weeks ago an undercover detective managed to land an advertised staff position inside your company, a pretty young woman who apparently gained almost unlimited access to everything and documented mountains of evidence—and, from what I hear, she doesn't think much of you, Kent."

"Suzie!" Kent gasped.

"And another detective posed as a naive but wealthy doctor," said the lawyer, "and recorded everything you said about an investment deal, right before the takedown—that was all they needed to make the arrest. He's the one who signaled the task force to move in."

"Dr. Cohen!" Kent choked in disbelief.

"Oh, yeah, Kent, before I forget," continued the attorney, "there's a longtime company employee, a guy who seems to know everything—he's cooperating with the whole investigation and has already made a plea deal to testify against you as a prosecution witness—says he got sick of always playing your stooge and never really getting all the good things you promised him."

"Jack!" cried Kent, now stricken with horror.

"Bail has been set at $250,000." The attorney spoke somberly. "And because this is such a complex case, I'll need a retainer of $100,000, just to get the defense started. I hope you've been squirreling away some money, Kent, because Kipp Konstruction Inc. is padlocked and out of business, and you could be facing many years of prison time. Oh, and I guess you didn't get to see the local TV news tonight—you're the lead story—CHRISTIAN BUSINESSMAN JAILED. It's funny, I never knew you were so religious, Kent, but they kept showing your company sign on the news and mentioning something about some Christian symbol you had on there, some fish or something—it's weird sometimes, what they consider newsworthy. Anyhow, Kent, since it turns out you're a Christian man, might I suggest that now would be a good time for you to do some serious praying?"

More Life Lessons—Bond Brothers Building

Brett Bond squinted as the late afternoon sun reflected off the long line of work trucks parked neatly in the lot beneath his office window.

"Sure," he said firmly, as he swiveled back toward the younger man seated across his desk from him, "construction is a tough way to make a living sometimes, with ups and downs in the economy, intense competition, and, all too often, everyone from owners and developers to bankers and politicians to suppliers and subcontractors all pressuring for a little something extra, a payment under the table here, a wink and a nod to shoddy work there, a kickback, a job for a relative, an inflated bid, a hidden substitution, a special favor. Sometimes we've even run into threats and intimidation, vandalism, and sabotage. There are days when it seems like the rest of the world has twisted the Golden Rule from 'Do unto others as you would have them do unto you' into something more like 'Just do whatever it takes.'

"But you know what? Look at all this, we've been through more than twenty-five years now, and here we are. We've done it all by the book—we've lost a lot of jobs we should have gotten, because we wouldn't play all the games, but in the end we've gotten so many good jobs from good people who've watched the way we work and know we're one of the few companies around that won't try to take them for a ride. We aren't the biggest company; we don't have the flashiest trucks or the best perks, but we make a good living. We take good care of our people, we try to honor God in everything we do, and I sleep well at the end of the day—and I really can't ask for any more than that. And your dad was such a big part of all this; so many times he was the one who kept me on the straight and narrow when I was almost ready to give in to temptation and go with the flow. Man, I miss that guy. I was blessed to have a brother like that. You were blessed to have a dad like that, Junior."

Brad Jr. had been listening to everything Uncle Brett said, pondering, wanting to do the right thing. It had been almost six months now since his dad, Uncle Brett's longtime business partner, Brad Bond Sr., had died unexpectedly. And a few weeks ago, Uncle Brett had called him with an unexpected invitation, asking him if he could come and spend a day or two with him on the job.

Brett and Brad Sr. had a written business succession plan. Brett had the legal option to buy out his deceased brother's share from the estate, and there was plenty of life insurance to make it happen comfortably and smoothly. If he wanted to, Brett was in a position to simply carry on the Bond Brothers Building legacy on his own. But Brett always tried to keep his eyes and his heart open for ways to serve God, and when he prayed about what to do with the business, he felt God was drawing him to Brad Jr.

Brad Sr. had always felt very strongly that Brad Jr. shouldn't work in the family business as a young man, because he had heard too many stories about owners' spoiled kids ruining companies and demoralizing the nonfamily employees, and Brett had always appreciated his brother's wisdom in that. And as for Brett, his own two daughters never showed the slightest interest in construction, so it wasn't really much of an issue with him. But now, Brad Jr., his brother's only son, was nearly thirty years old, with a wife and baby of his own. He had gone to college, working summers as a laborer for a construction company near the university. They liked him and after graduation offered him full-time employment there, promising him opportunity, but with the understanding he would have to work his way up from the bottom.

Now, nine years later, Brad Jr. had done just that. He was the company's chief estimator, probably the most critical job in the whole operation. But the company was family owned and there was little or no room for Brad Jr. to advance any further up the chain of command.

Brett liked what he saw in young Brad—a hardworking, knowledgeable man with a level head and a modest demeanor. In fact, Brad Jr. reminded Brett very much of his deceased brother, and it felt good to be around someone like that again. These last few months had been rough for Brett, leading the business alone after all the years of working so closely with his brother. And here, at Bond Brothers Building, the sky would be the limit for young Brad. He could take the company as far as Providence would allow, and well into the future past Brett's eventual retirement in another decade or so.

"Okay, Uncle Brett, suppose I am interested," asked Brad, "where would we go from here? What's the next step?" Brett looked hard into Brad's eyes and spoke carefully. "Brad, there's something I have to ask you. I know you'll give me an honest answer, but I need to make sure you understand the question. You see, your Dad and I were more than just brothers in an earthly sense, we were also brothers in spirit, brothers in Jesus Christ. That's more important to me than common blood. It runs even deeper, right down to the core of our hearts, why we do the things we do, and where we'll end up when this life ends—where your dad is now and where I'll be someday with him. And I'm very seriously considering offering you an opportunity to work your way into ownership of your dad's share in this business, but I need to know . . ."

"Uncle Brett, I think you can stop right there," Brad suddenly interjected. Brett felt his pulse quicken, fearing that young Brad might have been put off by the nature of his inquiry. But Brad continued, "I'll be the first to admit that maybe I was a little slow when it came to God and Jesus—you know, I heard that stuff all my life from my mom and dad—but somehow it didn't really register with me. And I'm sure you probably wonder about my high school and college days—I know I sometimes seemed really off track back then. I don't know how much my dad told you about me, but let's just say we had our struggles from time to time.

"But I have something to tell you, Uncle Brett, that I think you'll appreciate. You know, after college, there I was, young and single, working full-time, with no other responsibilities, with all the money I could spend—every night and every weekend free to do whatever I wanted. Well, you know how most of the guys on the crews are and I just fell right in with them—we pretty much looked for trouble wherever we could find it, drinking, drugs, women, you name it, we were living for it.

"But after a few months like that, I started feeling this sort of emptiness inside. I tried to drown it out at first, but it just kept coming back, stronger and stronger. And then words would just pop into my head, words I had heard from Dad, from our old preacher, from the counselors at church camp when I was a kid. I just couldn't escape—the emptiness and the words—no matter what I did to try to get away, for weeks it was all I could think about. After a while I didn't even want to go out in the evenings, it was like I was being gripped by some powerful force, something totally beyond my control.

"Somewhere I found my old Bible and I searched for the words that kept echoing in my mind—most of them turned out to be from the book of John and the book of Romans. And the next morning I had to go out real early to pull the tarp off a roof job we were working on, and I got out there right around sunrise, about an hour before the other guys, and I got that tarp all folded and I just sat there and watched the sun coming up with tears in my eyes. And I started to pray, for the first time since I was a kid, and I told God the truth, all the truth, and I asked for forgiveness and in that moment I trusted and believed that Jesus really had gone to the cross for me, for my sins, and that he really rose again to give me eternal life. And that was it, I was born again! I've never been the same since. So, yes, Uncle Brett, you may be my uncle, but you're really my brother!"

Brett's eyes were misting and he couldn't suppress his wide grin. "All right then, Brother," he exclaimed joyfully, "I think I have a proposal you're going to like!"

Biblical Insights

Do not steal. Do not lie. Do not deceive one another.—Leviticus 19:11

The mouth of the righteous man utters wisdom, and his tongue speaks what is just. The law of his God is in his heart; his feet do not slip. —Psalm 37:30–31

The wicked man earns deceptive wages, but he who sows righteousness reaps a sure reward.—Proverbs 11:18

Differing weights and differing measures—the LORD detests them both.—Proverbs 20:10

Simply let your "Yes" be "Yes" and your "No," "No"; anything beyond this comes from the evil one.—Matthew 5:37

You cannot serve both God and Money.—Matthew 6:24

Enter through the narrow gate. For wide is the gate and broad is the road that leads to destruction, and many enter through it. But small is the gate and narrow the road that leads to life, and only a few find it.—Matthew 7:13–14

Whoever can be trusted with very little can also be trusted with much, and whoever is dishonest with very little will also be dishonest with much.—Luke 16:10

Do not be yoked together with unbelievers. For what do righteousness and wickedness have in common? Or what fellowship can light have with darkness?—2 Corinthians 6:14

Practical Counsel

Some believers have probably never thought much about applying the principles of their Christian faith in their business dealings. Meanwhile, others are doubtless already immersed in the daily struggle to integrate Christian values with commercial enterprise. But do ethics really matter in the marketplace? Should doing business with Christians be different from doing business with anyone else? Are there "Christian business principles" that Christians should strive to abide by? History and experience teach us that *caveat emptor* ("Buyer beware!") is the number one rule of the marketplace. But is there a different standard, a place for God-honoring business practices?

Are Christians really supposed to accept and abide by the standards prevalent in the rough-and-tumble realm of commercial competition? Can we rightly brush off a promise with words like, "Hey, if it's not in writing, forget it"? Can we rightly send our employees out to face the world with cynical admonitions like, "Let's do it to them before they do it to us"? Can we rightly gloss over less-than-fully-honest dealings with meaningless catchphrases like, "Business is business"? Can we rightly absolve ourselves of responsibility for providing shoddy workmanship or substandard products with irresponsible excuses like, "It is what it is"? Isn't there a Christian alternative?

Scripture teaches that acquiring wealth through dishonest practices is unacceptable, that only the righteous earn a true reward. If we, as Christians, simply adopt the questionable business ethics prevalent in the world around us, then we are treading on dangerous ground with God. Regardless of what society tells us is okay, regardless of what everyone else seems to be doing, we need to be careful not to let greed lead us into treating anyone unfairly or deceptively. We need to focus on honoring and glorifying God in all aspects of our lives, including the way we do business with others.

Sometimes people react strangely when they find out I'm a born-again believer in Jesus Christ who actively practices law. I guess people think it's an oxymoron, like a square meatball, something that just doesn't make any sense: a Christian lawyer. But it makes sense to me because my primary call is to be a Christian, a disciple of Jesus. Everything else is second. It would be ridiculous if I claimed to be a Christian, but decided I was not going to be a Christian father to my kids or refused to be a Christian husband to my wife. And if we're going to be honest and authentic as Christians, then we have to bring our faith, our values, even Jesus himself, into every arena of our lives, including our jobs or professions, our business dealings, whatever we do. So as a believer, I have no legitimate choice but to bring Jesus into my law practice.

In Scripture, Jesus says, "Why do you call me, 'Lord, Lord,' and do not do what I say?" (Luke 6:46). I take that to mean we should try to obey God in all areas of life. In virtually every profession, trade, or business, obeying God will mean doing an honest job, working hard, treating people respectfully, and charging a fair price. If you're making widgets in a widget plant, maybe the actual end product won't be any different if you apply Christian principles to your work (but hopefully you'll still be a witness for Christ on the job and with your customers and your coworkers and your bosses and the maintenance crew and the security people and so on).

In other lines of work, like mine as an attorney, our products are often subjective and leave plenty of room for our Christian values to shine through in more obvious ways. For example, I believe that my legal advice should reflect not only what the local, state, and federal laws say, but what God's Word says as well. The stakes are simply too high to leave God out of the picture.

So what are some of the unique positive things that only we, as Christians, can bring into the marketplace, to be not only ethical, but to be a blessing to those whose paths we cross in the world of business? One of these is intentional prayer. We can pray for our associates, our employees, our employers and supervisors, our vendors and suppliers, our customers and clients, even for our adversaries and competitors! Imagine your entire business community transformed by the power of Christian businesspeople earnestly and consistently in prayer before God!

We can also focus on each person we come in contact with as a precious soul with an eternal destination, not simply another opportunity for us to profit financially. Jesus says, "You cannot serve both God and Money" (Matthew 6:24; Luke 16:13), and I think the biggest challenge for any Christian in business, for anyone with customers or clients or employees or suppliers or whoever it is we encounter, is to focus on the humanity of the people we deal with. It's too easy for any of us to start looking at dollar signs and forget that the person in front of us (or across town on the other end of a phone call or behind a computer on the other side of the world) is a real person with real emotion and pain, sometimes even with a real need to hear the message of salvation through Jesus Christ.

What if we change our focus from doing business transactions to doing *people* transactions? What if we focus on eternity? What if we focus on promoting healed hearts, reconciled relationships, and saved souls? What if we focus on bringing glory to Jesus Christ? The Enemy is trying to keep us thinking in terms of dollar signs, he's whispering to us to focus all our attention on making money. We need to fight back by looking beyond the dollar signs into the soul, focusing on people's eternal destinations, not their checkbooks.

And when we enter into any business or professional relationship, we need to be careful to remain faithful, even in the little things. As Jesus teaches, the way a person handles the little things reflects the way he or she will handle bigger things. So if we allow ourselves to be less than fair, less than honest, even in small matters, then those folks dealing with us had better take cover and hold on to their wallets when they entrust us with bigger matters!

As Christians toiling in the business world, we can also work faithfully to build up our credibility as witnesses for Christ by modeling integrity, good communications, and diligent work. If we can stay the course, when God's timing is right, we might be the one an unsaved person or a discouraged believer turns to when they need guidance in spiritual matters. And perhaps God will honor us with being the one to help lead a lost soul into his kingdom. But for that to happen, our lives in the workplace must be consistent with the beliefs we profess. Our actions betray what's really in our hearts, and we can talk a good game all day long, but if people don't see us living differently from the world, doing the things Christ commanded, then our witness becomes weak. People see we're all talk and no action. And nobody's impressed with an empty faith.

But the opposite is true as well. People, even the most cynical and jaded people we encounter in the marketplace, are deeply impressed when they see someone really living out their faith in the real world. When you have battle scars from standing up for

Christ and doing the things he commands, then even nonbelievers can't help but listen when you talk.

Even the way we conduct ourselves when we make a mistake or get drawn into sin can be a powerful witness to those with whom we do business. We're all human and we all fall short of the glory of God. Of course, we do the best we can, with God's help, to walk in the way of Christ. But when we fall, as we inevitably will from time to time, if we acknowledge our failures honestly, seek and receive Christ's forgiveness and the forgiveness of those we've offended, and then move ahead humbly, we can still draw those around us to Jesus. It's when we try to pretend we're perfect that we make poor witnesses, because people can see right through the facade.

We also need to consider whom we're doing business with, especially when an opportunity comes up to enter into a long-term business venture of some kind. Obviously, all of us are capable of making mistakes and even of acting sinfully toward one another. But, as Christians, we need to be especially cautious about getting closely involved in business ventures with folks who haven't surrendered their lives to Jesus Christ.

Now, please bear in mind I'm not trying to say all businesspeople who aren't born-again Christians are dishonest or unethical. In fact, I've observed nonbelieving businesspeople who are scrupulously honest and totally on the level with their customers and business associates, and I've observed Christian businesspeople who do shoddy work and take advantage of others. So why should going into business with nonbelievers be such a big issue? Does it really matter?

Apparently it matters to God, because in the Scriptures the apostle Paul specifically warns us: "Do not be mismatched with unbelievers. For what partnership is there between righteousness and lawlessness? Or what fellowship is there between light and darkness? What agreement does Christ have with Beliar? Or what does a believer share with an unbeliever?" (2 Corinthians 6:14–15 NRSV). More than anything else, I think God is encouraging us to be in partnership only with people who share our Christian worldview. The shared worldview is what's so essential, because even if a Christian is in partnership with the most honest, upright, competent nonbeliever, there will be times when their core values are in serious conflict.

For example, what if the Christian partner senses God's leading to start tithing from the profits of the business? That will be an awfully tough sell to his non-Christian partner! Or what if a dispute arises and the Christian partner feels called to settle the matter in a biblical way, through a Christian conflict resolution process, instead of through litigation in the courts? Again, this might be unacceptable to the non-Christian partner. Or what if a business opportunity comes up to make money from some legal but immoral activity or product that wouldn't be appropriate for a Christian to profit from? It might become a major source of discord and tension between the Christian and his or her non-Christian partner.

But isn't going into business together a good opportunity for the Christian to witness to an unbelieving partner? It may very well be so, and I realize God often works for the good in such circumstances, but for some reason, witnessing doesn't seem to be the primary emphasis in the Scriptures for this situation. I believe that sometimes we just have to *trust* when God tells us in Scripture to do something or not to do something. For that reason, I would be very hesitant to enter into any business venture with nonbelievers, even if it seems to make sense on the surface.

But no matter what business situation or arrangement we find ourselves in, the bottom line is for us to try to live out our Christianity right in the thick of the marketplace, so when we tell people about Christ, they'll already know a little bit about him by our actions. The only experience with Christ some people will ever have is the way we live our lives around them.

What if your employees have to tell their friends, "I work for a Christian, but the guy is a real jerk"?

What if your customers have to tell their friends, "I bought this from a Christian, but the guy really overcharged me"?

What if your suppliers have to tell their friends, "I have a contract with a Christian, but he's always late with his payments"? What a poor witness that would be.

The way our actions in the world of commerce impact our witness for Christ can be magnified (to the good or to the bad) when we choose to use the word "Christian" in our business name or advertising. Publicly displaying a Christian affiliation is something I've struggled with myself in my law practice. Certainly, I think it's vitally important for Christians to know there's a Christian attorney available, someone who understands and shares their faith, someone with similar moral and ethical values. But on the other hand, none of us wants to unfairly use or appear to be taking advantage of our faith in Christ as a tool to make money.

Scripturally, it's not an easy question. Jesus says, "Everyone therefore who acknowledges me before others, I also will acknowledge before my Father in heaven" (Matthew 10:32 NRSV). That tells me we need to be bold and public about proclaiming our faith in Christ in everything we do, including our businesses. But on the other hand, we have the account of Jesus driving the merchants out from the temple, saying, "'My house shall be called a house of prayer'; but you are making it a den of robbers" (Matthew 21:13 NRSV). That tells me we need to be very cautious in tying our businesses to the name of Christ.

Ultimately, I decided to publicly identify myself as a Christian lawyer. I worked out my decision prayerfully, in light of the Scriptures and, in the end, I felt I had no choice but to boldly proclaim the name of Christ in my law practice. But I cannot say every Christian businessperson needs to do the same thing. It's something each believer must work out before God "with fear and trembling" (Philippians 2:12).

But once we align ourselves with the name of Christ in the public arena, we face an even higher standard of accountability. We're all fallible human beings; we all make mistakes. Publicly associating ourselves with Christ in business puts us under greater scrutiny. It's a phenomenon similar to putting a Christian fish symbol on your car. Now you have to drive like a Christian, whether you want to or not, or risk bringing dishonor to Christ! It can be the same for a Christian in business. Claiming the name of Christ makes us more accountable to him in all we do, the way we treat our clients and customers, the way we treat our employees, our vendors, our competitors. Being under the banner of Christ forces us to consider everything more carefully. It makes us honestly ask ourselves, "Would Christ be pleased with the way I'm running this business?"

So I believe raising Christ's name in association with a business enterprise can be acceptable, provided it's not used as a means of gaining false trust for some corrupt or deceitful activity, and provided we remember constantly the bitterness toward Jesus and his church that will arise in the heart of a person who feels taken advantage of by someone trusted as a brother or sister in Christ.

God's Word never changes, yet it seems to become more relevant every day. And the importance of honesty and integrity in our financial and business dealings has never been more relevant. Over the years, many business leaders have successfully convinced themselves and others that honesty in the world of big business is nothing more than an old-fashioned notion, just not that important in today's fast-paced marketplace. But God has a way of humbling the arrogant! And the business landscape is littered with the smoldering ruins of major corporations and vast enterprises laid low by the moral and ethical failings of their "visionary" leaders, whose lack of honest dealing caused pain and loss for those who relied on them.

For those who would humble themselves enough to listen, God has made himself very clear. Here's just a sampling from the book of Proverbs alone! "The LORD detests differing weights, and dishonest scales do not please him" (20:23) . . . "Lying lips are an abomination to the LORD" (12:22 NRSV) . . . "Truthful lips will be established forever, but a lying tongue is only for a moment" (12:19 NASB) . . . "Great wealth is in the house of the righteous, but trouble is in the income of the wicked" (15:6 NASB) . . . "For the devious are an abomination to the LORD; But He is intimate with the upright" (3:32 NASB) . . . "He who profits illicitly troubles his own house" (15:27 NASB) . . . "The acquisition of treasures by a lying tongue is a fleeting vapor, the pursuit of death" (21:6 NASB) . . . "Wealth obtained by fraud dwindles" (13:11 NASB).

But even more important than all the warnings against dealing dishonestly, God also tells us, in the book of Romans, "Owe no one anything, except to love one another; for the one who loves another has fulfilled the law. The commandments, 'You shall not commit adultery; You shall not murder; You shall not steal; You shall not covet'; and any other commandment, are summed up in this word, 'Love your neighbor as yourself.' Love does no wrong to a neighbor; therefore, love is the fulfilling of the law" (13:8–10 NRSV). When we let Christ come into our hearts, one of the areas his Holy Spirit starts working on is our love for others. So, as professing Christians, if the only things preventing us from taking advantage of someone else are God's many warnings about dishonesty, then we need to examine our own hearts a little more closely. We need to pray that we will be delivered by God's grace to a place where we don't need any more warnings about cheating. We need to strive for a heart that cares so deeply about others, with Christ's genuine love, we would never even imagine taking advantage of them.

As Christians, God calls us to stand in the breach, to live out our faith boldly in the public square, even when it means confronting powerful forces of evil. But are we willing to do what's right? Whether we're an executive at the helm of a big corporation getting pressured by the shareholders to twist the truth in the annual report or a low-level employee getting pushed by coworkers to participate in petty theft of company property? When we're being asked to fudge the books a little in the accounting department? Or when we're being encouraged to make exaggerated promises to customers in the sales department?

Whatever it is in your workplace or business, I pray that God will fill you with the courage to stand in the breach, to do the right thing. After all, is it worth earning a good paycheck or handsome profit if you have to tell God to look the other way while you do your job?

CHAPTER 11

The Tax Dance

And he said to them, "Then render to Caesar the things
that are Caesar's, and to God the things that are God's."

—LUKE 20:25

Life Lessons—Alexey and Ariana

"What's this? What's all this paperwork? I pay my taxes!" shouted
Alexey, shoving a stack of papers and envelopes across the desk at his
accountant. "I work hard, I came to this country with nothing—
now I make money and pay plenty of taxes! I built my store
from nothing—isn't that what the government wants, isn't that
the American way?" Alexey was indignant.

"Alexey, you have a situation here, a real problem, a big mess,"
answered the accountant, "and I think you'd better hire yourself a
good tax lawyer, as soon as possible."

A few days later, Alexey found himself downtown, in a high-
rise office building, meeting with his new attorney, Henderson
Hendricks, a prominent taxation-law expert. "Mr. Andropov,"

Henderson began, "I've spoken at length with your accountant and my contacts within the Service—the Internal Revenue Service, that is. Let me summarize what I've learned from them and from the IRS notices you forwarded to me for review." Alexey looked into the attorney's eyes with irritation, but nodded for him to continue.

"Obviously, your business has been very successful, your revenues have increased every year. It's become quite an impressive enterprise," Henderson went on. "But there are certain indications, warning signs, 'red flags,' if you will, that the IRS looks for, ways they can cross-check information, methods they have for noticing whether your standard of living seems significantly beyond your reported income. In any event, the IRS has evidently now determined you and your wife have not been entirely forthcoming in your tax reporting."

Alexey's face reddened. "My wife? My dear Ariana? What's she got to do with any of this? She knows nothing of my business; she devotes herself to our home and children! I don't want her involved in any trouble with the IRS!"

But Henderson replied, "I'm sorry Mr. Andropov, but your wife signed all the joint returns you filed, so she is already every bit as much a target of the IRS as you are—and yes, both of you are in serious legal jeopardy—potential fines, potential imprisonment."

Alexey jumped to his feet. "Prison? That's crazy talk! Insane!"

"I'm afraid it's not so crazy, Mr. Andropov," Henderson continued in a calm, measured tone, hoping his client would follow his cue. "There are things that might not stand out, might not catch an examiner's eye when you are running a small mom-and-pop-style operation. But when a business grows the way yours has and you continue to do things the same old way, well, then you are practically begging for trouble."

Alexey slowly sat back down in the leather client chair, his voice beginning to quaver from the stress. "I don't understand, I only do the same things everyone else is doing. Isn't that the American way? Isn't that just business?"

"With all due respect, Mr. Andropov, I need to ask you some questions," said Henderson, looking over the pile of documents on his desk. "Is the allegation true you've been paying some of your people with cash right out of the registers?"

Alexey quickly defended himself. "Yes, but only the part-time and summer help, you know, the high school kids and the moonlighters—they appreciate the cash, without all those stupid payroll deductions—and for me it is a legitimate cost of doing business, so what's wrong with me spending my own money to pay my help?" Henderson listened quizzically. With his frustration mounting, Alexey then added without much thought, still trying to justify himself, "And this way I can pay a little less per hour and still attract the best workers, because it's all cash for them . . . tax-free."

"Uh-huh, and what about the payroll, Mr. Andropov?" Henderson asked, biting his tongue. "According to the records I have here, there are only two employees actually listed on the payroll, your wife and you—but don't you have floor managers, cashiers, buyers, stockroom people, bookkeepers, custodial crew? There are probably at least a dozen full-time people in most retail operations as big as yours, so where are they, why aren't they on the payroll?"

"Of course," Alexey replied, "we treat them as independent contractors—there is nothing wrong with that, every business I know of does it—and their income is reported to the IRS, every penny! And, again, you mention this matter of my wife. We must leave my beloved Ariana out of this. She knows nothing."

"Mr. Andropov, I wish I had the power to leave Ariana out of this, but that's not my decision—and right now she is up to her neck in legal problems with you," Henderson stated bluntly. "Both of you are in very deep trouble here. You've violated practically every payroll tax regulation there is by paying your part-time people with cash from the register—and you've probably put the IRS on *their* tails in the process. Plus, the IRS will certainly use this practice as evidence to prove you've been systematically understating your actual gross revenues, so they'll hit you with additional taxes due, fines, and penalties for all those years. Plus this whole independent contractor arrangement is almost sure to fall apart under scrutiny—if these people work regular hours set by you, get a fixed amount of payment for their work, use your equipment, operate by your rules, and so forth, then the IRS will probably retroactively reclassify all of them as regular employees, not independent contractors—and then your tax problems will be multiplied exponentially. Your legal situation will go from bad to worse."

"But don't I pay enough tax as it is? Why do they want more from me? Isn't this a free country?" Alexey protested. "Don't I have the right to run my business the way I choose?"

"Well," Henderson responded, "you certainly have the right to run your business within the law, but no, you don't get to decide how much tax is enough—the rules for that are set and the government expects everyone to comply with those rules. Now, I have one other question. What about that big bank loan you took out last year, for the renovation of the store and the purchase of the vacant land next door—when you applied for that loan, did you give the bank the same revenue and income figures you reported to the IRS on your tax returns?"

Alexey looked pained. "Look, everyone knows that what you tell the banker and what you tell the IRS are different stories—with the bank you must appear rich, with the IRS you must appear poor—so what?"

"Do you remember, Alexey," inquired Henderson, "that the loan you got was issued under a federal entrepreneurial development program, in connection with the Small Business Administration? Well, the feds are getting pretty sophisticated, and there's unfortunately a very good chance the information will be shared—you could be looking at loan fraud charges in addition to tax eva-

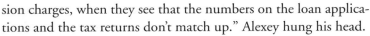

sion charges, when they see that the numbers on the loan applications and the tax returns don't match up." Alexey hung his head.

After a moment or two of silence, Alexey spoke again. "Okay, so now what, Mr. Big Shot Tax Lawyer, what do we do now?"

Henderson paused, then began to outline his counsel. "It's already late in the game. I wish you had come to me a year or two ago. We might have had a chance to voluntarily come clean and get everything straightened out without facing anything but some additional tax and penalties. But now the priority is going to be keeping you and your wife out of jail and, after that, saving your business, if that's still possible. I've been fairly successful in negotiating some reasonable deals for my clients in the past, even in some difficult situations like this one. But you and your wife are going to need to be fully cooperative, and it's going to involve some pain and probably some very high fines and penalties."

Alexey looked puzzled. Then he frowned, crossed his arms, and began to berate Henderson. "So we're just going to give up? You're a lawyer—aren't you supposed to fight for me? Fight for my rights? I thought you were the top gun around here—why can't you figure out some kind of a defense if you're so clever, if you're such a big tax expert? Isn't that what I'm paying you for?"

Henderson slowly shook his head and said firmly, "Mr. Andropov, I have won some very difficult cases for my clients over the years—big cases, complicated cases—I've been before the United States Supreme Court and won. Some of the cases I've handled are in the law school textbooks now. But in every one of those cases, there was a legitimate question of fact or law, there was a gray area, there was some reasonable basis upon which to expect that a fair judge would find that my client did not owe the taxes in question. Those are the kinds of cases we can fight and win.

"But what you have done is nothing more than garden-variety tax fraud. The facts are against you and the law is against you. You might think your ideas for beating the system were pretty clever, but I can tell you the people we are up against have seen it all before, the judges have seen it all before, and the outcome is essentially guaranteed. If we fight, we will lose. And you will face the worst of all the possible consequences. If we cooperate, there is still a chance for leniency. It's that simple. You can take my advice or leave it. But that's it. That's what you're paying me for. And I know exactly what I'm talking about here."

And with that, Henderson rose from his desk and began escorting Alexey from the office, explaining that he was due very shortly for a court appearance in another matter. Alexey said very little and Henderson offered a few parting words. "Naturally, the decision is ultimately yours and your wife's. I will represent you regardless of how you decide to proceed, and I will still get paid whether you end up negotiating a settlement or spending time in jail. In fact, I'll be paid more if we fight it all the way to the bitter end. But I'd suggest you think it over long and hard, and then let me know as soon as you can, no later than tomorrow morning. We don't have much time to lose."

And as Alexey rode down the elevator his thoughts turned to Ariana. *How will I inform her of this terrible news? How could this be happening to us? How could I have put her, my own wife, the mother of my children, at risk of going to prison? Has our American dream been shattered? God help us!*

More Life Lessons—Roland and Robin

"Mr. Rozetti, do you realize what would happen to a wad of cash like this at most small architectural firms?" asked Julie, the talkative new accounting clerk at Roland Rozetti Architecture LLC. "You know, I worked at a few different firms while my husband was going to school up north and the accounting managers always told me the same thing—when a client pays the owner for a job in cash, the money never hits the books. It's like that job never happened—it's like 'poof,' the money disappears straight into the owner's pockets. I guess a lot of business owners treat cash payments like some kind of tax-free gift. So how come you're bringing me this cash to deposit, Mr. Rozetti? Wouldn't you be better off to just squirrel it away, take your family on a little vacation or something?"

Roland Rozetti smiled as he replied, "Julie, maybe I'm a little different from the other people you've worked for—you see, I answer to a different authority, a higher authority . . ."

Julie interrupted, looking surprised. "Oh, I'm so sorry! I thought you were the big boss! I thought you were the owner! Now I'm so embarrassed! Please excuse me, I'm so sorry—you must think I'm so stupid!"

Roland's grin grew wider as he continued, "No need to be sorry, Julie. I'm the one who should apologize. Yes, my name is on all the paperwork, yes, I have all the titles, yes, I have the architect's license, and yes, the world sees me as the owner. But in reality, I'm not actually the boss here, I'm not really the owner."

Julie shook her head in slow comprehension as Roland went on. "The way I see it, Julie, I'm accountable to God for the way I live my life, the way I operate this business, everything I do. So God is the Boss, God is the Owner. I'm just taking care of things for him."

Julie began to chuckle, turning a bit crimson. "Boy, Mr. Rozetti, you probably do think I'm kind of stupid now. But I see what you're saying. I'm a believer in God also. I grew up going to church. But I'll tell you something, Mr. Rozetti, I've never seen anyone actually put God in charge of his whole life the way you do. And you seem to be so cheerful about it, like it's fun for you or something! I've never seen that before!"

Roland now turned a little red himself. "I appreciate your noticing, Julie. As far as I'm concerned, following God is a great joy. There is nothing I would rather do."

Julie laughed, then asked, "But how do you know what God wants you to do, especially when it comes to running an architectural firm? I mean I don't remember anything about that from Sunday school!"

Roland replied eagerly, "No, not every detail is in the Bible, but you'd be amazed how much there is. And for the things that aren't there, there is always prayer, asking the Holy Spirit to show me the way. My wife, Robin, and I pray for this business every week, that all of our decisions would be honoring to God. But when it comes to paying taxes fully and honestly, God left me such specific instructions, such clear policies to follow, I really don't have to do much praying about that at all."

"So, you mean there's something in the Bible about paying taxes?" Julie said curiously.

"Yes, one of the very specific policies God left me is that I'm supposed to pay all the taxes due—yes, it's right in the Bible, three times in fact—so I don't mess around with anything when it comes to taxes," Roland explained. "If we earn the money, I put it in the system, report it, and pay whatever taxes are necessary. And doing it that way sure keeps my life simple. I've never once had to worry or lose sleep fearing the IRS or any other taxing authorities. I wouldn't even worry if I got audited, because I know I'm 100 percent clean in all my tax stuff. And it's a great way to live. It's so peaceful to the soul."

"Okay," said Julie, "I guess that makes sense. It's just so different from what I'm used to. And I think I can totally see your point with real money, like this $2,500 you just handed me, but what about the other day when you handed me $5.46? Some silly little refund you got from the copy shop for printing expenses you had advanced for a client. Why in the world didn't you just stick that money in your wallet and keep it!? Do you realize that by the time I tracked down that account, made the deposit, and issued the refund check to the client with a letter of explanation, I had probably spent almost an hour of my workday? And you're paying me a lot more than $5.46 an hour!"

"It's all the same, Julie," Roland replied, "whether it's five dollars or five thousand or five million. God says to be faithful in even the little things. That money belonged to my client—it wasn't mine to keep. And if our books had showed us qualifying for a deduction for the full expense when really we had gotten a portion of it back, then we would have ended up paying a little bit less than we should have in taxes at the end of the year."

Julie shook her head. "Mr. Rozetti, it was five bucks and change! I'm sorry, but I don't think the IRS or anyone else would really care one way or the other."

Roland glanced at his watch and noticed it was almost time for him to meet his wife for lunch. "Listen, Julie, I've got to go meet Rachel," he concluded, "but consider this. By keeping everything on the up and up, even the small things—even the *smallest* things—everything takes care of itself. Everyone gets treated fairly—nobody gets cheated, not even the government. And you might think $5.46 is trivial, but I know from experience that refunding even the smallest amount to a client can be a powerful witness for our integrity as Christians, that it brings honor to Jesus."

"I will think about all that, Mr. Rozetti," said Julie as Roland began to head for the door, "and when you get back from lunch, can you tell me where you and Robin go to church? It's been a while for me and we really should find a church down here now that we're all moved in. And if the people at your church are anything like you, I'm kind of curious to check it out! Oh, and have a great lunch!"

Over lunch, Roland spoke enthusiastically, "You won't believe it, Rach. I was talking with that new girl, Julie, in accounting, the one you helped me hire. I get the sense that she knows there is a God, but I'm not so sure she's a born-again believer. But now she and her husband are thinking about coming to check out our church!"

Robin smiled. "Roland, you are such a gifted evangelist—how did you find out so much about her spiritual condition, and how did you get her so interested in coming to our church?"

Roland laughed, "Well, it's a long story, but basically it's because I refuse to cheat on my taxes!"

Biblical Insights

A fortune made by a lying tongue is a fleeting vapor and a deadly snare.—Proverbs 21:6

"Tell us then, what is your opinion? Is it right to pay taxes to the Caesar or not?" But Jesus, knowing their evil intent, said, "You hypocrites, why are you trying to trap me? Show me the coin used for paying the tax." They brought him a denarius, and he asked them, "Whose portrait is this? And whose inscription?" "Caesar's," they replied. Then he said to them, "Give to Caesar what is Caesar's, and to God what is God's."—Matthew 22:17–21

Then Jesus said to them, 'Give to Caesar what is Caesar's and to God what is God's.' And they were amazed at him.—Mark 12:17

Practical Counsel

There are few subjects Jesus addresses so directly and bluntly as the matter of paying taxes. And the perspective of Jesus, the genuine "Christian perspective" if ever there was one, is simple: Pay the taxes you owe. And it's repeated in three of the four gospels. There is no question that the law and Christian teaching, the teaching of Jesus himself, are perfectly aligned on this issue. And it would appear this teaching is broad enough to apply to taxes of every variety, whether income taxes, sales taxes, transfer taxes, property taxes, capital-gains taxes, death taxes, or otherwise, and whether the taxes are federal, state, or local.

Yet many Christians inexplicably seem to struggle with honesty and full compliance when it comes to paying taxes. And some Christians continue to dance around the issue of taxes almost as if they believe there is an entirely separate standard of morality that applies, as if the distinction between lies and truth mysteriously evaporates in the realm of taxation.

And, yes, some attorneys, both Christian and otherwise, are all too willing to accommodate or even enable the deception. But in my experience, taxation is one area of the law in which most lawyers actually tend to push their clients toward greater honesty and more complete compliance with the law. Whether this arises from a sense of ethics or merely from a keen awareness of the dire consequences likely to befall a tax-evading client (and possibly his attorney), it is a phenomenon I have repeatedly observed and even experienced myself in counseling clients.

For reasons not entirely comprehensible, clients will present me with their creative "home-brewed" schemes for evading some tax (almost always the schemes ultimately boil down to not reporting income or not disclosing the existence or true value of assets involved in a transaction or estate—in other words, outright fraud) with the apparent expectation I will willingly facilitate their planned dishonesty. And sometimes the reaction of clients (sadly, even otherwise upstanding Christian clients) is one of anger and indignation when they learn I will not cooperate and will, in fact, insist on full compliance with the applicable tax laws.

It is important to note, of course, there is a huge and fundamental difference between tax avoidance and tax evasion. The first is perfectly legal and ethical, the second is a crime and a breach of Christian ethics. Tax avoidance means lawfully applying knowledge of the tax laws in order to minimize tax consequences—that is, using the very laws of the emperor, the laws of Caesar, the laws of the government levying the tax in question, to the fullest advantage as a citizen. Tax avoidance might mean anything from making sure to report every lawful deduction to diligently planning to qualify for every legitimate credit to carefully investing in only the most tax-favored types of investments. But tax avoidance works fully within the parameters of the law. It is essentially the precise calculation of what is actually due Caesar, leaving no stone unturned, paying not one dollar more than is required. Tax evasion, on the other hand, involves minimizing taxes by breaking the law. Tax evasion is ripping Caesar off.

And while on occasion there might be some "gray areas" in the field of tax law, places where techniques some attorneys interpret as legitimate tax-avoidance tools are instead interpreted by the tax authorities as tools of unlawful tax evasion, in my experience that is not where most Christians are encountering problems. Unfortunately, the problems I tend to become aware of fall squarely within the categories of tax issues that are totally black-and-white. And they typically involve a desire by the client to outright cheat the government of taxes that would otherwise be due. In other words, a desire to directly contradict the teaching of Jesus on taxes.

In many cases, Christians seem susceptible to buying into the common worldly perspective that if the government doesn't know about something, then it's not taxable. That principle is nowhere to be found in the law or the Bible. Neither Jesus nor the tax laws make an exception for cash income! Nonetheless, many people I've encountered, churchgoing, born-again Christians among them, seem to be convinced that if they manage to receive cash income, they need not report it on their tax returns.

Likewise, in situations where assets will be subject to taxation, such as in the administration of the estates of deceased persons, there seems to be a prevailing notion that the heirs are well within their rights to hide whatever they can from the government and undervalue the rest. I have sometimes encountered an almost brazen attitude of deception in these kinds of circumstances. And, of course, the cases of intended fraud I have become aware of are probably only the tip of the iceberg, as I would naturally have to imagine that many of the folks who intend to deceive the government in estate cases probably know better than to tell their lawyer about the things they are trying to hide.

Another commonly encountered "culturally acceptable" attempt at tax evasion arises in situations where a sales tax or other transfer tax is due, usually in the context of an exchange of personal property or real estate. For example, I have been personally pressured by the buyer of a used vehicle I was selling (pressure which I wisely resisted) to underreport the sales price of the vehicle on official state forms, in order to reduce the amount of sales tax the buyer would have to pay. I was literally told by the buyer, "Everybody does it," as if that were a valid excuse. And I have been surprised by requests to accommodate similar attempts at outright tax evasion in various forms in my role as legal counsel handling real estate transfers and other transactions. And again, the people in question have as often as not been churchgoing Christians, people who might otherwise make every effort to live by the scriptural exhortation to avoid being conformed to the standards of our fallen world.

And perhaps the most prevalent form of attempted tax evasion I observe is the effort by many employers to improperly classify their actual employees as nonemployee independent contractors, in order to "beat the system" and avoid all the various payroll-related tax obligations. But again, there is no exception in the law or in Scripture that says Christians need not render unto Caesar that which is Caesar's if it will be inconvenient for them, making the administration of their business more onerous. It seems to me (and I know this to be the established position of virtually all taxing authorities!) that taxes due are taxes due, regardless of how annoying or burdensome they may be.

Sometimes, Christians also run into legal or spiritual issues when it comes to properly claiming tax deductions, such as those for charitable giving generally permitted on federal income tax returns to offset taxable income. And while this book is not intended to be a tax guide, the primary rule of thumb for such tax deductions is to make sure they are all fully documented in compliance with the applicable law and regulations. And just as with respect to other potential forms of tax evasion, claiming phony or inflated deductions of any kind is both legally and morally unacceptable for a Christian taxpayer.

But even with respect to otherwise perfectly legitimate tax deductions, Christians sometimes struggle over whether it is really appropriate for them to claim a tax deduction for their tithes and offerings to Christian ministries. The concern arises from Scripture passages like the one found at Matthew, chapter 6, verses 3 and 4: "But when you give to the needy, do not let your left hand know what your right hand is doing, so that your giving may be in secret. Then your Father, who sees what is done in secret, will reward you." So, is claiming a deduction for the amount of your donations on your tax return really the same as telling the world about it, rather than just keeping it between you and God?

In Matthew 22, Jesus is asked about paying taxes to the government. He says, "Give therefore to the emperor the things that are the emperor's, and to God the things that are God's" (v. 21 NRSV). What that indicates to me is we must pay our taxes to the government in accordance with the government's laws. In our country, our government has specifically made laws that allow us to reduce the amount we owe in taxes based on our giving to charities, including Christian ministries and churches. So on the one hand, the Bible tells us not to flaunt our giving, not to show off for public display. But on the other hand, we are told to pay our taxes in accordance with the law, and the law allows us to take a deduction for our giving.

In a situation like this, I believe each individual Christian must pray and search God's Word for wisdom, to confirm that your choice is right in God's sight. As for me, since the only people who look at most tax returns are unknown IRS employees in another city somewhere, I don't feel like I am showing off by taking a deduction for my giving. I strongly suspect that the people who review our returns could care less what we give, as long as we are honest in our reporting. And to me it's good stewardship to pay only the taxes required by law, not any extra. But at the same time, I would certainly respect the decision of a person who has prayerfully considered the issue and feels it wouldn't be right to list all his or her giving on a tax return, especially if that person is sensing the kindling of inappropriate pride in revealing their giving habits to even an anonymous IRS employee. If he or she finds peace with God in keeping all giving totally anonymous, then that too is a blessing.

CHAPTER 12

The Real Estate Push

Nothing is covered up that will not be uncovered, and nothing secret
that will not become known. Therefore whatever you have said
in the dark will be heard in the light, and what you have whispered
behind closed doors will be proclaimed from the housetops.

—LUKE 12:2–3 (NRSV)

Life Lessons—Max and Mindy

"Who are you?" the stranger on the front porch demanded impatiently. "What are you doing in my house? And why won't my key work? What in God's name is going on here?"

Mindy's mind spun with confusion at the stranger's words, but finally she shot back, "Huh? Who am *I*? What I want to know is, who are *you*? And why are you trying to open our door? Are you some kind of maniac? I'll have my husband call the police if you don't get off our porch right now!"

"Look," the stranger insisted, "if you won't let me in my own house, then you tell *my* husband to get himself out here and talk to me now. What are you, his little girlfriend or something? I knew he was up to no good!" At that moment the stranger tried to peer inside past Mindy, catching a glimpse of stacks of moving boxes. "Oh, my God!" the stranger screamed, "where's my stuff? What is going on? Are you robbing my house? I'm going to call the police if you don't let me in or bring my husband out here right now!"

Mindy was incredulous, unable to make sense of anything the stranger was saying. Regaining some composure, Mindy tried again. "Okay, look, lady, I don't know who you are or what your problem is. Why do you think your husband is inside my house? And why do you think we have your stuff? Is this some kind of joke? Is there a hidden camera somewhere? Because if you're serious, you're really starting to scare me."

Now the stranger was becoming visibly agitated, her face turning red, her clenched fists trembling. "I'm Patricia Peterson," the stranger shouted. "This is my house, 2719 Canary Court. What, do you want to see my driver's license or something? Should I get a neighbor to vouch for me? To get inside my own house—now come on, this is ridiculous!"

Max had overheard the commotion from upstairs and now joined Mindy in the doorway. "And who are you?" the stranger shrieked at Max. "Did Paul invite the whole town into our house? Now where is he? Paul! Paul! Paul! Get out here now!"

Max was as baffled as Mindy, but then something registered in his mind, pieces falling into place as he said, "Paul . . . Peterson . . . Paul Peterson . . . Paul and Patricia Peterson! We met them at the real estate office yesterday! Paul and Patricia Peterson! They were the owners; they sold us this house! So you have something to do with the former owners? Are you related or something? They don't live here anymore—they moved out of state I think—maybe the real estate agent could help . . ."

But at that moment the hysterical stranger cut him off. "You're crazy! *I'm* Patricia Peterson! And I can assure you, I don't know you! And I didn't move anywhere—I just got back from a week taking care of my elderly parents upstate and now I'm home, here, at my house, 2719 Canary Court, where I live, where I've lived for four-teen years, and where I intend to keep on living, if you two would please get out of my doorway!"

The loud confrontation on the porch soon drew the attention of neighbors, several of whom called the police. Within the hour, formal statements were being taken, identification documents were being checked, and puzzled officers were huddled in heated dis-cussion. Finally one of the police officers requested that Max, Mindy, and the purported Patricia Peterson join him for a chat near his patrol car. "Look, folks," he began, "this is one of the strangest calls I've ever worked. Everything checks out—every-thing—the story about the real estate agent and the settlement yes-terday—it checks out. And, as far as I can tell, this really is Patricia Peterson—her ID checks out and all the neighbors recognize her. But here's the kicker—when I talked with the real estate agent, I asked him to describe Patricia Peterson, and he said she was a petite redhead, kind of flashy, maybe about 35 at the oldest . . . no offense, Mrs. Peterson, but that doesn't sound a lot like you."

Patricia's jaw tightened. "It's that girl Paul knows from down at the dealership where he works, one of the receptionists. She was in the middle of a long, nasty divorce. I had a bad feeling about her, and I just knew Paul was up to something. But with me being gone every other week caring for my folks, I couldn't really keep an eye on things. Well, isn't that great? She pretended she was me. At least that explains some things, like the weird questions one of the neighbors asked me a month or two ago about when I was moving—Paul must have been quietly showing the house on the weeks I was away. So, Officer, now that we know what happened, will you please tell these people to get out of my house? It's very late, I have to do some serious thinking, and I'm exhausted."

Max and Mindy had been listening in horrified sympathy to Patricia's plight, but her last comment caught them off guard.

"Hold on now, Mrs. Peterson," Max quickly interjected. "We just spent everything we had, signed two mortgages we won't be able to pay off for thirty years if we're lucky, and maxed out our credit cards, all to buy this house!"

"Plus we're in debt to my uncle for the money he kicked in to help us swing the deal," added Mindy adamantly, "and besides, it's not like we have anyplace else to go—our apartment lease ran out yesterday and this is our home. We paid for it fair and square."

All eyes were on the police officer. "Folks, all I can tell you is I'm not going to charge any of you with trespassing tonight. And if you can give me the name of that redhead, Mrs. Peterson, I'm gonna see about getting an arrest warrant issued for her, on theft by deception charges. But beyond that, sorting all this out is more of a civil matter and you're gonna have to talk to your lawyers about that," the officer said matter-of-factly with a shrug of his shoulders.

"Now I've got more urgent things for my guys to handle, so I'd suggest you go ahead and work out some temporary arrangements for tonight." And after a minute or two more of awkward and unproductive discussion with Max and Mindy under the officer's impatient gaze, Patricia reluctantly accepted an offer of lodging for the night from a neighbor.

The next morning found Max and Mindy at the office of a local real estate attorney, Keith Krupp, Esquire, where they breathlessly raced through their tale of woe. Krupp asked a few questions along the way and took notes furiously. When they had finished, Krupp took his turn to speak, reviewing the situation and some of his observations.

"So, the real estate people told you there would be no need to have an attorney involved in the whole house-buying process? That's unfortunate, because having a guy like me on your side from the beginning might have saved you a lot of heartache," Krupp said, shaking his head wistfully. "But that's water under the bridge now. Okay, let's see, so the house was a little above your original price range, but you loved it and your agent told you he might know a way to pull it off for you. You didn't quite understand his explanation but he suggested you just do things his way and not ask too many questions, that it would all work out.

"Then he had you sign a purchase contract for a price substantially higher than what the sellers were asking and also a separate little private side agreement that said the sellers would repay you for the part of the purchase price above the asking price right after the closing. Then the agent introduced you to the mortgage broker, who told you with a wink not to worry, that the appraiser was a good friend of hers and that there was little doubt in her mind the appraisal would come in high enough. And the mortgage broker also told you to provide her with a letter from your uncle saying the money he was lending you was really a gift.

"And then, when the real estate agent called a few days before the scheduled settlement with some final figures and you realized you weren't going to have enough cash to cover all the closing costs and insurance, he told you to go ahead and take out cash advances on your credit cards, since the mortgage company had already completed all its credit checks and they wouldn't find out about it now.

"Then, at the closing the day before yesterday, nobody asked for photo identification from you or the sellers, and you don't remember a notary being anywhere in the room. And then, when all the papers were signed and Max started trying to remind the real estate agent about the private side agreement, the one that said the seller was supposed to pay you back for part of the purchase price, the agent kicked Max under the table and talked like you must have gotten mixed up about something, so you just shut up and played dumb. And later, after everyone else had left, the agent handed you a simple personal check from the Petersons for the thousands of dollars they owed you, signed by Mrs. Peterson on a joint account at a local bank. Is that pretty much it? Am I leaving anything out?"

Max and Mindy didn't like the way their story sounded as Krupp reflected it back to them in his own words, but, "Yes," they agreed, "that's pretty much it in a nutshell." Then, almost simultaneously, Max and Mindy said, "The check!" Max continued, "We didn't even get a chance to take that check from the Petersons down to the bank yet—yesterday was so hectic. We were planning to deposit the check and use that money to pay off most of the cash we advanced on our credit cards for the closing. You don't think it's a bad check, do you?"

Krupp stared at his desk for a moment, then replied, "I'm sorry, but you two don't really think it's a *good* check, do you? If Paul Peterson didn't drain that account for the road before he and his little friend left town, then I guarantee that the real Patricia will close it out today—and either way, I don't expect the signature of 'Patricia Peterson' on that check will match the one on the bank's signature card. No, I think you can kiss that money good-bye."

"But we're broke then, flat broke. I don't even know how we're going to be able to pay you for your legal work," Mindy said with trepidation. "But at least we get to keep our house, right? I mean we paid for it, it's ours, right? Right?" Mindy was alarmed when Krupp didn't offer immediate reassurance.

"I'm afraid it's not all that clear yet, Mindy," said Krupp. "You're in the middle of quite a tangled web—there's now a deed on record with a fraudulent signature, and the real Patricia Peterson isn't going to just give up on her house that easily—and no one knows where the money you paid 'the Petersons' has gotten to, but presumably it skipped town with Paul and the redhead.

"Your purchase contract stated a bogus price to induce the mortgage company to loan you more than their lending ratios should allow, and you cooperated in helping keep that fact hidden from the title insurance agent at settlement. Your appraisal was apparently rigged, arguably with your knowledge. You reported the loan from your uncle as a gift. And you maxed out your credit cards before signing the final loan documents, without disclosing it to the mortgage company. Meanwhile, you signed two promissory notes, for the primary mortgage and the second instant home equity mortgage, and your payments on those are going to start coming due in a month—that's if you're lucky and the bank doesn't accelerate the payments as soon as they find out about this mess."

Krupp then wrapped things up: "Folks, if I were a meteorologist, I would predict you're about to experience a litigation storm—both civil and criminal actions—and in some of the cases, you may very well be the defendants. You're going to see everyone involved try to pass the buck to each other: real estate agency, individual agents, appraiser, lender, loan officer, notary, mortgage underwriter, title insurer, and, of course the Petersons—both real and counterfeit—and the law enforcement agencies and lending regulators. And, yes, I'm going to need a very substantial retainer if you want me to represent you in all this." Shaken to the bone and afraid even to ask what Krupp meant by "substantial," Max and Mindy just sat in silence.

More Life Lessons—Stu and Shari

Stu and Shari looked at each other and laughed, both feeling as if a great burden had been lifted from their shoulders. "It's so funny that something this obvious would have taken us so long to figure out!" Stu exclaimed.

"Yes," Shari agreed, "how hard should it be for us to realize that we ought to live within our means? It doesn't get much more basic than that! But somehow all that talk about 'Here's how much house you can afford' and 'Here's how much money you can qualify to borrow on a mortgage' is kind of seductive—it draws you right into thinking biggest and most, instead of modest and sensible."

"I'll tell you what," replied Stu, "I feel like a prisoner who's just been granted his freedom! Just think about the possibilities. If we buy a smaller place, maybe something we can afford on just one of our salaries, then we can do so much more in life—we can travel, we can save for retirement, we can give more generously to church and charities—and maybe someday, if God blesses us with children, we can afford to have you stay at home and be a full-time mom, instead of being forced to go out and work to pay the mortgage like so many moms, with the kids stuck in some day care!"

"The word 'sustainable' comes to mind," said Shari, "instead of being stuck on a treadmill, stuck in the rat race, I think we can live a more relaxed life, embrace a saner and more sober pace. Sure we can keep working as hard as we want and maybe even save for a bigger place someday if that's what we decide, but what's the rush? Why put ourselves under so much pressure? It's crazy! And to think, we almost got pushed right into the trap!"

"Yeah, that real estate agent of ours sure did sound pretty disappointed when we told him we decided not to make an offer on that big new place outside of town," Stu recalled. "But now that we understand a little better how this game is played, doesn't it seem a little suspicious that he would always insist on taking us to the higher-end places, the ones we could barely afford. Or even the ones just out of our reach, almost like he was conditioning us to think that way, training us to think the smaller places were somehow unworthy of our consideration?

"It seems to be the way the whole real estate industry works—the agents, the lenders, the builders, even the lawyers and the title insurance agents—they all do better, they all get a bigger cut when the price is higher. So they all have a vested interest in keeping the buyers thinking big! And I think most of our society has bought right into the sales pitch—just look at the size of all the new houses going up. Almost nobody can afford them without both spouses working full-time."

Shari gave Stu a warm hug. "Stu, thank you so much for considering my opinion when I asked if you'd be willing to spend a day of prayer, fasting, and Scripture reading before we made a final decision on that big house. It was a huge decision that was going to affect the way we lived for possibly the rest of our lives. I really felt it deserved special attention, it really deserved to be committed fully to God, and not just with lip service, but with serious prayer. I know you really wanted that house. I know it was hard for you to let go and listen for God's leading."

Stu smiled and said, "Shari, I should be thanking you. God showed me so much hidden pride within my heart. God stripped away so many delusions and false idols I had unknowingly permitted to take hold of my thinking. I don't think I really even wanted that house; I think I just wanted to prove to the world I'm a success. I think I wanted a symbol to show off—how ridiculous is that for a born-again Christian man with the best wife in the world? Like I need to prove anything to anybody! I needed a good, strong dose of humility, and that day of prayer was God's way of reaching my stubborn heart. So thank *you*, Honey!"

"How about if we do something to commemorate and celebrate our newfound freedom?" Shari asked. "Could we maybe take a decent chunk of that money we've been fanatically squirreling away for the huge down payment we thought we were going to need? Could we maybe use it to make a special donation to the home-repair ministry our church does every summer?"

Stu was nodding enthusiastically. "Amen, Sister, what a perfect idea! God is helping us build our house, so why don't we honor him by helping him build *his* house! This whole house hunting thing is really starting to get fun!"

Biblical Insights

Unless the LORD builds the house, its builders labor in vain.—Psalm 127:1

Fields shall be bought for money, and deeds shall be signed and sealed and witnessed, in the land of Benjamin, in the places around Jerusalem, and in the cities of Judah, of the hill country, of the Shephelah, and of the Negeb; for I will restore their fortunes, says the LORD.—Jeremiah 32:44 (NRSV)

LORD, you have assigned me my portion and my cup; you have made my lot secure. The boundary lines have fallen for me in pleasant places; surely I have a delightful inheritance.—Psalm 16:5–6

I love the house where you live, O LORD, the place where your glory dwells. Do not take away my soul along with sinners, my life with bloodthirsty men, in whose hands are wicked schemes, whose right hands are full of bribes.—Psalm 26:8–10

Everyone lies to his neighbor; their flattering lips speak with deception. —Psalm 12:2

The house of the wicked will be destroyed, but the tent of the upright will flourish.—Proverbs 14:11

Woe to you lawyers! For you have taken away the key of knowledge; you did not enter yourselves, and you hindered those who were entering. —Luke 11:52 (NRSV)

Practical Counsel

Purchasing a home remains, for most people, the largest single investment they will ever make. And the homes we purchase often end up as central features in our lives, the stages upon which life's dramas unfold for us. We make not only a major financial investment, but also a huge psychological investment in our real estate. And the manner in which we choose to purchase a home will often define our lifestyle for years or decades to come. Will we live with moral and financial peace, or will we struggle with the burdens and consequences of being morally compromised and financially overextended? And, whether we're buying or selling or financing real estate, will we remember to glorify Christ in the process, or will we push him aside until the deal is done?

The world of real estate is full of axioms and a cast of often colorful characters. "Location, location, location" is, of course, the most famous axiom. And the stereotyped pushy, overly eager real estate agent, willing to do whatever it takes to make the sale, is still a common part of the landscape. And the world of real estate is also full of money, often big money, and all the temptations and questionable schemes that such financial opportunities invariably seem to produce. The recent subprime mortgage loan crisis is just one example of how irrational greed can overwhelm good sense in the real estate market. Unfortunately, when it comes to real estate, the ill-advised subprime lending and borrowing fad wasn't the first moral meltdown and it won't be the last. The temptation to bend or ignore the rules is just too great for too many people.

Probably the most useful advice I can provide for the Christian who is planning to enter into any sort of real estate transaction is to consider carefully where the loyalties of the professionals they will rely upon for assistance are really directed. In other words, are the real estate agent, the loan officer, the title insurance agent, the appraiser, the home inspector, the lawyer loyal to *you* or merely loyal to the *transaction* itself? When you consider the fact many of these people and the companies they work for won't make a dime unless the deal closes, the question answers itself. And even those who get paid whether the deal closes or not often rely on a steady stream of referrals from those who make their money strictly from completed transactions, so they can't afford to gain a reputation for standing in the way of business as usual. There is immense and pervading pressure on everyone concerned to keep the wheels greased, to "close the deal" at all costs.

Once we grasp where the real loyalty of the people "helping" us is often focused, we won't be so prone to passively allowing them to substitute their moral judgments for ours. We can be on the alert for opportunities to put our own faith and morals into action, even if our decisions are perceived as "rocking the boat," "making things difficult," or "being a stickler."

So, what might this look like in the real world? Well, it could mean a Christian couple selling a piece of property is careful to scrupulously disclose every defect of which they are aware, even when the real estate agent is urging them to gloss over things that might interfere with quick and easy marketing. Or it could mean the Christian first-time home buyer refuses to fudge any detail when completing the mortgage loan application, even when they are reassuringly told that "everyone does it," even when it means the mortgage might not be approved and the deal might fall through. Basically, it means being prepared from the beginning of the process to refuse to abandon the ethical and moral high ground in exchange for convenience and expediency.

And while Christ-honoring morals should be the most important factor in determining how a Christian conducts himself or herself in a real estate transaction, it should be noted that the long and persistent history of fraud, deception, and dishonest conduct so often prevalent in real estate matters has given rise to a complex web of federal and state laws and regulations designed to keep things strictly on the up and up. Laws regulate many aspects of not only the real estate transaction itself, but also the related banking and insurance and brokerage arrangements. Common illicit practices include (but are not limited to) concealing latent defects, misrepresenting financial terms, sharing commissions and fees without disclosure (kickbacks), identity fraud, and "flip transactions" (involving a series of conveyances in which the price is artificially inflated). These activities can and often do lead to civil actions and damages, and sometimes even to criminal fines or jail time for those involved.

But even the Christian who enters the realm of real estate transactions with strong morals and the best intentions of abiding strictly by the law can still become a victim of unscrupulous operators. Sometimes the individual parties, especially those with less sophistication and experience, are intentionally taken advantage of. For example, abusive and predatory lending practices by financial institutions targeting unsuspecting borrowers continue to occur. In simple terms, lenders sometimes knowingly offer mortgage loans with terms that make it virtually impossible for borrowers to repay them; then, when the inevitable default occurs, the lenders move in quickly with a blizzard of legal action and seize the property for resale at a handsome profit.

In other cases, the lending arrangements offered aren't necessarily illegal, but they still put the unsophisticated consumer into very difficult financial circumstances. For example, many real estate lenders will accommodate buyers who cannot afford a traditional down payment by offering them a regular first mortgage and an immediately effective second mortgage, or home equity loan, so 100 percent (or sometimes even more) of the home's value is financed from the moment of purchase. If real estate prices in that geographic area happen to decline, the owners will then find themselves "upside down," or "in the bucket," on the house, unable to sell the property because they owe more on it than the proceeds of a sale will generate after all the commissions, taxes, and other costs of sale are deducted from the price.

Given the multiple opportunities for legal and ethical standards to be pushed to the limit and beyond, and the distinct possibility of unfair and deceptive practices being thrust upon the unsuspecting consumer, seeking the counsel of a truly knowledgeable and unbiased independent legal adviser would seem to be an obvious first step for anyone contemplating a real estate transaction of any kind. But sadly, all too often, one of the first things the consumer will be told by the industry insiders is "Oh, you don't need a lawyer—that will just cost you extra—we'll take care of everything. Don't worry about it, we do this all the time."

And for the consumer who persists in desiring legal representation, too often they will be steered by the real estate professionals right into the arms of a "friendly" law firm or lawyer, someone with a track record of going along to get along, possibly even someone with an off-the-record referral-fee arrangement or some other vested interest in the outcome.

In real estate, the stakes are high. The potential risks and rewards are great. And for many, the terrain is unfamiliar. Christians contemplating involvement in any type of real estate matter are well advised to start with a healthy dose of prayer and a long reading of Scripture (the book of Proverbs is the perfect place to be morally refreshed and reminded how God-fearing Christians should live out their faith in the realm of worldly business). This should be followed by a visit to a wise and ethical real estate attorney who shares their values and will help guide them through the process, endeavoring to protect them from the many pitfalls and temptations that lie ahead.

CHAPTER 13

The Christian Conciliation Alternative

Blessed are the peacemakers,
for they will be called sons of God.

—MATTHEW 5:9

Life Lessons—Eldon and Emily

To Eldon, it all seemed to make sense at first. The way he saw it, his customer didn't pay him for work he did. He tried everything he could think of to get the customer to pay. When nothing else worked, he had his lawyer file a lawsuit to collect the money. It wasn't even that much money in the grand scheme of things, but for a small building contractor like Eldon, it was enough. Not receiving the money made it difficult for Eldon and his wife, Emily, to stay current with some of their bills, made it necessary for them to put off a planned week at the beach, and made Eldon angrier and angrier whenever he thought about it.

But on the day Eldon signed the papers to finalize the lawsuit, he never dreamed that within a few months the situation would have cost him and Emily several lifelong friends and caused their church to experience an ugly and painful congregational split.

"I still don't get it," said Eldon with frustration. "I don't see why old Hoover won't just pay the money he owes me for that job!"

Emily looked at Eldon and shrugged. "Hon, neither do I. He's a stubborn man, a proud man. I guess he still blames you for the water damage from the broken pipe . . ."

Eldon raised his voice. "Emily, I told you, that pipe had nothing to do with me! It was an old pipe and it was just a coincidence that it busted while I was on the job!"

Emily paused, then asked, "Eldon, is that the way you reacted when Hoover first asked you to pay for the water damage?"

"What do you mean, Emily?" Eldon demanded. "Sure, I told him in no uncertain terms it wasn't my fault and that I wouldn't think of paying for the damage—and that was the truth. What else was I supposed to say? He was just plain wrong! But, boy, I wish I knew then that he was going to blame me anyway, and that he was going to let me finish my work and then refuse to pay me! I would have walked off the job that very day if I had only known, but I thought I could trust a fellow Christian, an elder of our own church! Who knew the guy would turn out to be a liar and a coward!"

Emily tried again. "But don't you see, Eldon, you didn't give him much of a chance to talk things out with you—maybe there's something to that story he told the pastor about the wires you'd been running getting caught on the old solder joint and breaking the pipe loose."

"No way, no way!" Eldon shot back. "I don't even want to hear another thing about Hoover and his crazy lies! And I still can't believe he was going around telling that phony story to our pastor and the other elders behind my back—calling me a liar when I wasn't even there to defend myself! I'm a professional and I know my trade, and I know I didn't damage that pipe! I have my reputation to protect! And that's why I had to write to the elder board and the pastor, that's why I had to set the record straight about Hoover and all the lies he was spreading about me!

"And to think, that young pastor had the nerve to come over here and get in my face about me calling Hoover a liar and a coward in my letter! And then for him to give me that pious lecture about how the Bible says Christians shouldn't sue fellow Christians! Well, I wonder how he feels about it now that there's not enough money in the offering plate to pay his salary, now that so many of our friends have left the church with us!"

Emily had a sad look on her face. "Eldon, doesn't it bother you some of our friends didn't leave the church with us? There were some good people, old friends, people I'll really miss. And all the memories."

Eldon frowned and told her, "Forget about 'em. If they want to side with that no-good Hoover and his cronies on the elder board, then let 'em. But they're no friends of mine!" Eldon looked at Emily's face and noticed she was tearing up. "Emily, just think— the trial is coming up in only a few weeks. We'll have our day in court; we'll prove Hoover is a lying deadbeat. And we'll show that pushy pastor he's wrong! Justice will be done and we'll get the respect we deserve! And we'll get our money!"

Emily's tears began to flow. "I don't know, Eldon, I just don't know if I care about the money or any of this anymore. I just wish there was some way to go back to the way things were . . ."

More Life Lessons—Ronnie and Reba

Ronnie and Reba sat down at the small table in the private conference room. "You know, Ronnie," Reba said in a surprised tone, "I hate to admit it, but there might be something to this Christian conciliation business after all. What's your take on the offer they've asked us to consider?"

Ronnie couldn't conceal the grin forming on his face. The Christian mediation session had lasted about two hours. There were some heated words at first, but as things went on there were also some times of heartfelt sharing, some tears, and even some laughter. Now, after a few minutes of silent prayer with everyone still sitting around the big table, the mediator had asked Ronnie and Reba and the couple they'd been having so much trouble with (Mr. and Mrs. Davis) to adjourn to separate waiting areas, while she prepared a settlement proposal she hoped would be acceptable to both sides. And she had just returned to the small conference room with that proposal, which she handed to Ronnie.

Ronnie and Reba had been struggling back and forth with their new neighbors, the Davis's, for several months, mostly by way of tense and unfriendly phone messages. The trouble started one day while Ronnie and Reba were at work, when the Davis's constructed a high wooden fence between the two properties. The concept of a fence was fine with Ronnie and Reba—in fact, Ronnie and Reba themselves had often talked about installing a fence along the back of their yard for better privacy—but money was tight and the project was always deferred. The problem was that the Davis's new fence encroached on Ronnie and Reba's property by several feet, cutting off their access to part of their own yard.

Thinking at first that it was a simple mistake that could easily be taken care of if the Davis's were informed of their error, Ronnie and Reba tried stopping at the Davis's house to talk on several different evenings after work, but no one ever answered their knocks on the door. After several failed attempts at a personal visit, Ronnie was becoming a bit edgy about the situation and was able to track down the Davis's phone number. Reaching a voice-mail system when he tried to call, Ronnie let his increasing frustration get the best of him and left a rather confrontational message with instructions for the Davis's to correct the problem immediately. After another week or so of inaction, Ronnie, now even more frustrated, called again, leaving an even more insistent message. But again there was no response.

From time to time Ronnie and Reba could see lights or other signs of activity at the Davis house, but whenever they would call, the voice-mail system was all they could reach. And when they again attempted a personal visit, there was still no answer at the door, even though they could hear music playing inside. And the fence remained in place.

Now Ronnie and Reba were becoming convinced the Davis's were intentionally ignoring the situation. Finally, after another week or so, Reba came home from work to find a message on their own home answering machine from Mr. Davis. He sounded upset and said his wife had been emotionally shaken by hearing the "threatening" messages left by Ronnie, and insisted Ronnie stop calling her. And things only worsened from there, as several more hostile messages were exchanged, with various denials and further accusations being issued by the husbands.

The tone of the messages eventually prompted Mr. Davis to contact his lawyer for assistance, and a few days later an attorney's letter addressed to Ronnie and Reba arrived, warning them to cease and desist from their "harassment" of the Davis's. The letter did not even mention the fence. Ronnie was incensed and called his own lawyer the next morning, arranging to meet with him and bring him the letter later in the week.

When the appointment finally arrived, Ronnie and the attorney talked about the whole situation at some length. The attorney and Ronnie had first met when they were serving together on the board of a local Christian charity some years ago, and that sparked an idea in the lawyer's mind.

"Ronnie," he suggested, "I can write you a big scary letter and shoot it back at the attorney for the Davis's, disputing all their charges, making our own countercharges and, of course, bringing up the whole issue of the fence. But experience tells me such a letter is likely to lead merely to another letter from opposing counsel, going on the record to deny our allegations, and so on and so forth until we work something out through some long and expensive negotiation process—or we end up in court, fighting things out at even greater expense. And when it's all over, you will still be living as an enemy of your neighbors." Ronnie acknowledged the lawyer's comments with a nod.

"I recall you are a Christian man, Ronnie," the lawyer continued, "and, if I have my facts straight, I also recall Jesus saying something about us loving our neighbors. And, frankly, I'm tired of watching the legal system turn neighbors into enemies, and I'm tired of being a part of that ugly process.

"There's a new organization in town called the Christian Conflict Resolution Center. I met their chief mediator at a local bar association function the other week. She seems very well qualified—she's a lawyer with extensive specialized training in alternative dispute resolution from a Christian perspective. Her goal is to resolve disputes in a biblically based manner so at the end of the process, the adversaries will not only feel justice was done, but they will be fully reconciled into fellowship with each other—all with God's help, I might add! And I found out about her rates, too—I can promise you, if she's as effective as she appears to be, you will save yourself a substantial sum in legal fees if you use her services.

"So what do you think, Ronnie? Want to give it a shot? If you say 'yes,' I'm quite sure I can persuade the attorney representing the Davises to make a similar recommendation to them. Of course, they would have to agree to meet with the mediator to make any of this work."

After some discussion and persuasion, Reba agreed with Ronnie that they ought to give this Christian mediator a chance to see what she could do, especially since it might save them some money. Ronnie let their attorney know and he got the wheels in motion. It turned out the Davises were receptive to the concept, being active Christian believers themselves. And soon the day came for the mediation session.

The facts and circumstances the mediator was able to draw out of the parties put everything in a different and unexpected light. It turned out that within days of his family's move into the new house, Mr. Davis, an engineer, had been assigned by his employer to troubleshoot a major industrial installation project overseas. The assignment was for forty-five days, and he had not been home to supervise the fence installation. In his absence, Mrs. Davis had been sketchy on the precise whereabouts of the lot line, leading to the unintentional error in the placement of the fence. And because of his overseas location, Mr. Davis had extremely limited communication with his wife and could only call home occasionally, and never during the evenings when Ronnie and Reba were usually home.

Mrs. Davis worked the evening shift as a nurse at a local hospital, sometimes leaving her thirteen-year-old daughter home alone, always with strict instructions not to answer the phone or open the door for anyone during her absence. Mrs. Davis had become overwhelmed with the unanticipated responsibility for settling into the new house in her husband's absence and had fallen behind in checking her phone messages and other usual household responsibilities.

The Davises were now expressing a willingness to make immediate arrangements for the removal of the fence to the proper boundary line at their own expense, provided Ronnie and Reba would apologize for their antagonistic tone in communication throughout the matter.

And the mediator's settlement proposal that Ronnie and Reba were now reviewing was the reason Ronnie couldn't hold back his smile. It contained five points: (1) Ronnie and Reba would sign a note of apology to the Davis's for their conduct, (2) the Davis's would likewise sign a note of apology for *their* conduct, (3) the

Davis's would cause the fence to be promptly relocated to the correct boundary at their own expense, repairing any damage to Ronnie and Reba's yard, (4) Ronnie and Reba would, within the next thirty days, have the Davis's over for a backyard barbeque at their home, and (5) the Davis's would reciprocate with a barbeque of their own within thirty days of Ronnie and Reba's cookout.

"I say we take the offer!" exclaimed Ronnie.

"Amen!" agreed Reba. "It's a deal!"

Biblical Insights

When any of you has a grievance against another, do you dare to take it to court before the unrighteous, instead of taking it before the saints? Do you not know that the saints will judge the world? And if the world is to be judged by you, are you incompetent to try trivial cases? —1 Corinthians 6:1–2 (NRSV)

Therefore, if you are offering your gift at the altar and there remember that your brother has something against you, leave your gift there in front of the altar. First go and be reconciled to your brother, then come and offer your gift.—Matthew 5:23–24

Do nothing from selfish ambition or conceit, but in humility regard others as better than yourselves. Let each of you look not to your own interests, but to the interests of others.—Philippians 2:3–4 (NRSV)

But I tell you who hear me: Love your enemies, do good to those who hate you, bless those who curse you, pray for those who mistreat you. If someone strikes you on one cheek, turn to him the other also. If someone takes your cloak, do not stop him from taking your tunic. Give to everyone who asks you, and if anyone takes what belongs to you, do not demand it back. Do to others what you would have them do to you.—Luke 6:27–31

So watch yourselves. If your brother sins, rebuke him, and if he repents, forgive him. If he sins against you seven times in a day, and seven times comes back to you and says, 'I repent,' forgive him.—Luke 17:3–4

The LORD is compassionate and gracious, slow to anger, abounding in love. He will not always accuse, nor will he harbor his anger forever; he does not treat us as our sins deserve or repay us according to our iniquities.—Psalm 103:8–10

If another member of the church sins against you, go and point out the fault when the two of you are alone. If the member listens to you, you have regained that one. But if you are not listened to, take one or two others along with you, so that every word may be confirmed by the evidence of two or three witnesses. If the member refuses to listen to them, tell it to the church; and if the offender refuses to listen even to the church, let such a one be to you as a Gentile and a tax-collector.
—Matthew 18:15–17 (NRSV)

As a prisoner for the Lord, then, I urge you to live a life worthy of the calling you have received. Be completely humble and gentle; be patient, bearing with one another in love. Make every effort to keep the unity of the Spirit through the bond of peace.—Ephesians 4:1–3

So whether you eat or drink or whatever you do, do it all for the glory of God. Do not cause anyone to stumble, whether Jews, Greeks or the church of God—even as I try to please everybody in every way. For I am not seeking my own good but the good of many, so that they may be saved. Follow my example, as I follow the example of Christ.
—1 Corinthians 10:31–11:1

Practical Counsel

How can we provide for disputes to be resolved in a manner that honors God? Is there a realistic alternative to lawsuits and other litigation? God wants us to honor him in all aspects of our lives, including those inevitable personal and business disputes. God's Word provides us with clear guidelines to help us resolve conflicts in a way that glorifies him. And, in stark contrast to the secular legal system, God's way challenges us to seek the interests of others as well as our own, with a focus on preserving relationships, not "winning at any cost." A biblical approach to conciliation addresses underlying factors involved in disputes and provides a genuine opportunity for true justice and healing.

A Christian mediation and reconciliation process can be pursued simply and informally by seeking the assistance of a trusted brother or sister in Christ to help disputing parties talk through and resolve their differences, or it can be pursued formally by involving the leadership of the church or a professionally trained Christian mediator. Either way, Christian dispute resolution can spare everyone involved the misery and expense of litigation in the secular courts, while providing a much more satisfactory conclusion and a Christ-honoring witness to the watching world. And, thankfully, there are now numerous individuals and organizations throughout the country with ministries specifically devoted to facilitating Christian mediation and reconciliation. Some mediators are Christian attorneys, some are Christian counselors or social workers, some operate under the umbrella of nonprofit organizations, and some are extensions of traditional church pastoral ministries and denominational agencies.

The process of Christian dispute resolution may unfold in various ways, depending upon the history of the conflict, the stage at which assistance is sought, and the complexity of the underlying matter. In some cases, the mediator may undertake an independent investigation of the facts and circumstances, while in others the mediator may simply bring the parties together in a neutral environment for facilitated discussion and negotiation. In every case, the matter will be bathed in prayer and the Scriptures will be opened for relevant guidance. Typically, the mediator is not empowered to make a binding decision, but rather will diligently seek to guide the parties into a mutually acceptable resolution, some uniquely crafted outcome both parties can willingly embrace.

Of course, Christian conciliation is usually a realistic alternative only if both parties are willing to become involved in such a process. (Any individual embroiled in a dispute would surely benefit from receiving trained Christian peacemaking counsel, even if the other party refuses to partake. In some cases that counsel might even include some effective strategies for encouraging the reluctant party to join in the process in spite of misgivings or skepticism.) And, yes, the common Christian faith of the parties is also normally a prerequisite to commencing a Christian reconciliation process, although there have been instances where even a non-Christian is willing to consider giving Christian arbitration or mediation a try.

One excellent way to ensure that any possible future disputes between Christian parties involved in a formal ongoing relationship (for example, landlord and tenant, employer and employee, buyer and seller, homeowner and contractor, business partners, etc.) will be resolved through a Christian conciliation process, rather than risking the unnecessary stress, expense, and unbiblical aspects of secular court litigation, is to include a Christian conciliation clause in the underlying legal agreements governing the relationship (lease, employment contract, sales agreement, construction contract, partnership agreement, etc.). The inclusion of such a clause is also a clear witness to others that you trust in God and desire to follow his principles in every aspect of your life. In simple terms, the Christian conciliation clause would state that if an unresolvable dispute arises between the parties, they agree in advance to submit the problem to biblically based Christian mediation or arbitration (binding or nonbinding, as the parties see fit) and to abide by the outcome of that process.

In addition to their use in contractual documents, Christian conciliation clauses can also be adapted for use in estate-planning documents, such as wills and trusts, to encourage positive, God-honoring, relationship-preserving resolution of any disputes that might arise among heirs in settling an estate. Other applications of Christian conciliation clauses might include corporate bylaws, organizational rules, church governance documents, and the like.

The Bible strongly discourages us from getting involved in litigation. God knows the heavy toll a lawsuit can take on our finances, our families, and our emotions. And getting involved in a lawsuit can distract us from doing the truly important things in life, the things that will build up God's kingdom. Our witness of Christ to the world can really suffer from our involvement in litigation. So choosing voluntary Christian conciliation and advocating for the use of Christian conciliation clauses are ideal ways for Christians to stand up for Jesus and stand against the culture of unhealthy, destructive dispute resolution in which we find ourselves immersed.

Chapter 14

A Contract with God (An Invitation)

For God so loved the world that he gave his one and only Son,
that whoever believes in him shall not perish but have eternal life.

—JOHN 3:16

Life Lessons—Exchange of Promises

As a lawyer, I am often called upon to document contracts for my clients. For example, if someone says to my client, "If you give me fifty thousand dollars, I'll give you my land"—that's what we call an "offer" in legal jargon. And let's suppose my client wants to buy the land at that price, so he says, "Okay, I'll give you fifty thousand dollars for the land"—that's what we call "accepting the offer." Once an offer is accepted, there is an agreement, a meeting of the minds, a contract. Some contracts must be in writing, others can simply be informal oral agreements. But the essence of a contract is the mutual consideration, the give and take, the "I'll do this if you'll do that." At the core, a contract is a binding exchange of promises.

I know lawyers sometimes look at things a little differently, but did you know that the Bible is full of contracts? Of course, not everything in the Bible is a contract. Some things God tells us in the Bible are simply unilateral promises, where God just gives us certain things without asking us to do anything in return, like his promise never again to flood the entire earth. Some other things God tells us in the Bible are laws, where God forbids us from doing something or requires us to do something, like most of the Commandments. Some other things in the Bible are simply God's good advice, like many of the proverbs, basically God telling us, "Here's a better way." And some things in the Bible are expressions of worship or love, such as many of the psalms.

But throughout the Bible, there are also many contracts, places where God tells us, "If you do something, I'll do something for you in return"—a basic legal contract.

And of all the contracts God proposes to us in his Word, there is one I consider to be especially important. So important, in fact, God provided for it to be mentioned in numerous places throughout Scripture, presumably so we might have ample opportunity to consider and accept this very special offer. One place this offer appears, where the terms of this proposed contract with God are laid out before us, is in Romans, chapter 10, verse 9: "Because if you confess with your lips that Jesus is Lord and believe in your heart that God raised him from the dead, you will be saved."

This offer from God is clear and concise. God doesn't rely on complicated terminology or confusing "weasel words" such as you might find in a contract written by lawyers. Instead he simply tells us, "If you confess and believe, I'll save you."

And to make God's proposal into a binding contract, all we have to do is accept the offer. Once we've accepted the offer, it's a done deal. God doesn't say, "If you confess and believe, you *might* be saved" or "If you confess and believe, I *might* consider saving you *if* you're good enough from here on out." God's contract is very simple, with no loopholes. If you confess and believe, you *will* be saved!

If you've never entered into this contract with God, I humbly encourage you to "sign on the dotted line" right now. This is the best and most priceless legal advice you will ever receive from any lawyer.

If you're ready in your heart to accept the terms, to receive your eternal salvation, I beg you to pray these words, whoever you are, wherever you are, at this very moment: "Jesus Christ, you are the Lord, the Son of God, the only Savior of mankind, *my* Lord, *my* Savior . . . and Jesus, I believe that you died on the cross for me, an imperfect sinner, to spare me the punishment I deserve, and that God really did raise you from the dead, and that you're really living with God your Father in heaven . . . and God, I accept your offer of salvation."

Amen. May God bless you abundantly!

Appendix:
Helpful Resources

Plans fail for lack of counsel, but with
many advisers they succeed.

—PROVERBS 15:22

Helpful Resources and a Gift for You from the Author

Visit the author's helpful Web sites at www.IsThereALawyerInThe
Church.com and www.practicalcounsel.com to dig deeper into God's
Word on the legal situations you face, and to learn how you can
arrange to have Attorney Bloom share more of his encouraging, equip-
ping, and challenging teaching on Christianity and the law directly
with you or your organization. And don't forget to click the "Readers" link on either Web site to request a special free gift of appreciation and encouragement just for you, the readers of this book!

Other Helpful Resources Online

Advocates International: www.advocatesinternational.org

Alliance Defense Fund: www.alliancedefensefund.org

American Association of Christian Counselors: www.aacc.net

American Center for Law and Justice: www.aclj.org

Center for Law and Culture: www.lawandculture.org

Christian Law Association: www.christianlaw.org

Christian Legal Society: www.clsnet.org

Church Law and Tax Update: www.christianitytoday.com/lyris/cltupdate/archives/

Crown Financial Ministries: www.crown.org

International Justice Mission: www.ijm.org

Justice Fellowship: www.justicefellowship.org

National Christian Foundation: www.nationalchristian.com

National Legal Foundation: www.nlf.net

Peacemaker Ministries: www.peacemaker.net

Thomas More Law Center: www.thomasmore.org

Will to Live Project: www.nrlc.org/euthanasia/willtolive